# THE CONSTITUTION

*Reflection of a Changing Nation*

# THE
# CONSTITUTION

*Reflection of a Changing Nation*

## MARGOT C.J. MABIE

HENRY HOLT AND COMPANY

NEW YORK

*For James*

Published by Henry Holt and Company, Inc.,
521 Fifth Avenue, New York, New York 10175.
Distributed in Canada by Fitzhenry & Whiteside Limited,
195 Allstate Parkway, Markham, Ontario L3R 4T8.

Library of Congress Cataloging in Publication Data
Mabie, Margot C. J.
The Constitution: reflection of a changing nation.
Bibliography: p.
Includes index.
Summary: Presents the text of the Constitution and
examines its origins, ratification, and amendments and
how the document reflects the changing character of
the nation.
1. United States—Constitutional history—Juvenile
literature. 2. United States. Constitutional
Convention (1787)—Juvenile literature. [1. United
States—Constitutional history. 2. United States.
Constitutional Convention (1787) 3. United States—
Constitution] I. Title.
KF4541.Z9M25 1987    342.73′023    86-33502
ISBN 0-8050-0335-5    347.30223

First Edition
Designed by Susan Hood
Printed in the United States of America
10 9 8 7 6 5 4 3 2 1

ISBN 0-8050-0335-5

# CONTENTS

# PREFACE

Americans celebrate the Fourth of July with exuberance. We unfurl our flags. We decorate floats and don marching-band uniforms for the parades that wend their way through the streets of big cities and small towns across the country. We consume countless hamburgers, hot dogs, and watermelon slices. We gasp as fireworks bloom into chrysanthemums against the dark night sky.

Celebrating the signing of the Declaration of Independence, we celebrate the birth of our nation. But strictly speaking, the Declaration of Independence announced the birth of thirteen sovereign states. The real birth of our nation took place on September 17, 1787, when delegates to a Federal Convention in Philadelphia finished writing the Constitution of the United States. The terms of that constitution called for the states to give up some of their sovereignty—the power to make and enforce all of their own governmental decisions—to a national government.

For nearly four months, delegates from twelve states—Rhode Island sent no representatives—labored on the document. Proposing, debating, holding firm, compromising, giving way, the delegates who took part in the convention* eventually agreed on an outline, or frame, for our national government. The Confederation Congress, which had called the convention, sent the Constitution to the states for approval by the people. Just as envisioning a national government required a leap of imagination on the part of the framers, agreeing to the establishment of that government

*For a list of delegates and the states they represented, see page 103.

required a leap of faith on the part of the people. Vehemently debated, the Constitution was narrowly approved—indeed, it is generally conceded that a minority of Americans in 1787 favored the adoption of the Constitution.

For twentieth-century Americans like you and me, the Constitution hardly seems revolutionary. Its preamble is restrained; its seven articles and, now, twenty-six amendments make for dry reading. The Constitution proclaims no high ideals, makes use of no rhetorical flourishes. But its businesslike prose is deceptive, for it masks the Constitution's theoretical basis. Man's place in the universe, his role in society, his very nature—these are questions that have engaged thinkers for millennia. The framers were well versed in the political writings of philosophers, from the ancient Greeks, Plato and Aristotle, to Locke and Montesquieu. Further, the framers were accustomed to thinking politically because of their recent struggle with England; they had fought for American independence on the grounds that England had violated their constitutional rights as Englishmen. They believed in God, and they believed that an organized society provided the best milieu in which man could come to understand and fulfill God's plan. But they believed, too, that man, with his incomplete understanding of God, could be evil. Recognizing the need for a strong national government and fearing the evil that comes when power is abused, they invented a system of government that is, first, limited; that government could concern itself only with certain issues. Second, the limited powers of that government would be parceled out to separate branches, each with its own mechanisms for braking the other branches. Hedged by those balances and checks, the government could not exceed its limits. The Constitution's terse outline of the scope and workings of the national government represents the first of the modern constitutions; never before had a people set down in writing a clear, comprehensive statement of the role and powers of their government. And never before had people with their own governments—in this case the sovereign states—agreed to the establishment of yet another, higher government.

What is literally marvelous about the Constitution of the United States is that the original document, with the addition of twenty-six amendments, continues to serve as the nation's political blue-print. We look to the Constitution to see if today's laws, written for today's United States, conform to its strictures. We even look to the Constitution to amend the Constitution. Like the Americans of 1787, we wrangle about the role of government, how it works and how it should work. But unlike the Americans of 1787, our debates begin with the terms—some firm, some vague—and the silences of the Constitution. Accepting the basic principles, we often disagree about how to apply them. Therein lies the liveliness of the document. Enduring debates, vigorous debates, are but a reflection of our enduring, vigorous Constitution.

# THE
# CONSTITUTION

*Reflection of a Changing Nation*

# 1

# THE CONFEDERATION

The conflict between England and her colonies in America that eventually erupted into the American Revolution began brewing in 1763. Having vanquished the French and Indians in the Seven Years' War, England was faced with a national debt swollen by the cost of that war. Further, there would be expenses for the administration and defense of the enormous territory—Canada and the land between the Appalachian Mountains and the Mississippi River—gained through victory. The British estimated that they would need some ten thousand soldiers to keep the Indians and French in line. To the British, it seemed only appropriate that the colonists should pay for their own defense. Parliament, in London, would levy taxes.

The prospect of a standing British army alarmed the colonists. Many believed that the British really wanted to control the colonists, that the French and the Indians were merely an excuse to introduce troops. But the prospect of being taxed by Parliament, where the colonists had no representatives, rather than by their own assemblies, was even more alarming. Considering themselves loyal subjects, the colonists would spend more than ten years defending their rights as Englishmen, while Parliament insisted on its right to levy taxes directly.

John Dickinson's draft of the Articles of Confederation and Perpetual Union (The Historical Society of Pennsylvania)

The colonies, each with its own charter from the Crown and its own assembly, dealt directly with the mother country; they had at that time no political forum in which to discuss among themselves their individual and collective grievances with the king and Parliament. But through letters and newspapers they kept abreast of events in and responses by other colonies. The fundamental issue—taxation without representation—concerned all the colonies equally. And when Parliament punished one colony, the others knew the same could happen to them.

In the fall of 1774, Americans created their own political forum. The First Continental Congress, with representatives from all of the colonies, met to consider how to resolve their quarrel with the mother country. The relationship was not to be saved. England and her American colonies went to war.

The Congress appointed George Washington commander in chief of the Continental Army. The name suggests one large army, but in fact it was closer to thirteen individual armies working in concert. Each state enlisted, equipped, and paid its soldiers. Washington and the Congress might request certain numbers, but they could not require the states to meet those figures, and as it turned out, the states never did meet them. The war was run on a shoestring; indeed, after the Battle of Yorktown, when the British finally surrendered, there was no money to pay a messenger to take the good news of the war's conclusion to the Congress.

During the war, the states formalized their relationship. The Continental Congress drew up the Articles of Confederation and Perpetual Union, a document specifying the matters the states would handle collectively, as a league, and the procedures by which that confederation would function. Approved by the Continental Congress on November 15, 1777, the Articles of Confederation were then sent to the state legislatures for ratification—that is, approval of an agreement concluded on one's behalf by all parties involved. Maryland, the last to sign on, ratified on February 27, 1781; the Continental Congress declared the document in force and became the Confederation Congress on March 1, 1781.

The Confederation was entirely in keeping with the temper of the times. It reflected the desire for union that grew out of all that Americans shared—their heritage from and complaints with England. At the same time, the Confederation reflected a desire for autonomy; having experienced England's heavy-handed use of power, Americans were leery of a central authority that might not be attentive to their particular interests. Americans gave their allegiance not to the United States but to their own states—John Adams spoke of Massachusetts as "our country."[1] Only because of the war did the states band together to set up a confederation.

The Articles of Confederation provided for a single legislative, or lawmaking, body to deal with foreign powers, wage war and make peace, and coin money. There was no executive—no person or group charged with carrying out the measures decided on by the legislature. Nor was there a judiciary—that is, there were no judges presiding over court cases. Expenses of the Confederation were to be met by contributions from the states, contributions determined on the basis of land values. As in the Continental Congress, each state had one vote in the Confederation Congress. Some measures required unanimous approval by the states in order to pass. The others required what is called an extraordinary majority—that is, well over half; the Confederation Congress set its extraordinary majority at two-thirds, or nine states. The larger states—Massachusetts, New York, Pennsylvania, and Virginia—believed that congressional votes should be apportioned on the basis of a state's population, but the small states insisted that each state have an equal share in the decision-making.

In keeping with the concept of confederation, Article II held that "Each state retains its sovereignty, freedom and independence." The Confederation Congress had the power to make decisions on all manner of issues, but with Article II, it had no power to enforce those decisions. Congress had to rely on the voluntary cooperation of the states, but the states did not always find it in their own interest to cooperate.

The states had held together sufficiently to win the war. But with the peace, the glue that bound them together was dangerously thinned. The states, proudly asserting their sovereignty, freedom, and independence, refused to go along with some of the decisions of the Confederation. Further, they began bickering among themselves.

There were problems with foreign powers. Congress had appointed John Jay head of a commission to negotiate the peace treaty with England. Among the agreed-upon provisions were two that the states would not honor: payment of prewar debts owed by Americans to British merchants, and payment for property that states had seized from Tory sympathizers during and after the war. Congress could not enforce the provisions of the Treaty of Paris.

The Confederation's problems with England were not confined to diplomacy. Nor were they all caused by the Americans. Some Englishmen hoped, for sentimental reasons, that the ties between the mother country and the states might be restored. Others longed for the prosperity that trade with the Americans had provided before the Revolution. To ensure the health of the economy at home, England passed the Navigation Acts in 1783. They required that all goods moving between the states and the British West Indies be transported on ships built in England, owned and sailed by Englishmen. American ships could carry goods to England so long as those ships carried goods produced only in the state in which the shipowner resided.

The intention was to limit the states' foreign trade to England. It made no difference that the acts might create ill will between England and the states. The English knew that Americans needed British goods. They also knew that the Confederation Congress had no power to regulate commerce. Even if it did, the states were unlikely to adhere to whatever policy Congress might decide on. Some Englishmen thought that if enough pressure was brought to bear in the area of commerce, the states would slip the loose bonds of their pathetic confederation and return, one by one, to the British fold.

Manufacturers would have liked Congress to act. Manufacturing had not been strong during the colonial period, for England had protected its own manufacturers in the mother country by holding down manufacturing in the colonies. With the war concluded, American manufacturing was ready to bloom, but the development of new industries was impeded by the lack of tariffs—charges on foreign goods brought into the states.

With Congress unable to respond to the Navigation Acts, many states took matters into their own hands. New Hampshire, Massachusetts, Rhode Island, New York, and Pennsylvania passed their own navigation acts aimed against the English, whereupon Connecticut invited English shipping to its ports. The Confederation Congress did consider a single navigation act for all the states to use, but some southern states refused to endorse the plan. With no shipping of their own, Southerners feared that Northern shippers, free of competition from the English, would set sky-high rates to transport the South's tobacco and rice.

Some Americans feared that such a display of impotence in Congress and disunity among the states might whet the appetite of England, as well as France and Spain. At the time, those were the three most powerful nations, and all had a presence on the American continent. For each, dominance over the weak states would significantly alter the balance of world power.

The Confederation also had severe problems at home. To begin, there was the war debt. To finance the Revolution, bonds had been sold. By these, money had been borrowed, with the obligation to repay that money, with interest, at a later date. When the war ended, Congress could not raise the money from the states to pay off the debt, or even to pay the interest on it. (In 1789, Alexander Hamilton, as secretary of the treasury, would estimate that Congress owed over $40 million in principal and interest to Americans alone.[2]) So low was the confidence in Congress's ability ever to redeem the bonds that speculators, gambling that Congress might honor the obligation, could buy the bonds for as little as one-twentieth of their face value.

Another area of speculation, one that dated from before the Revolution, was the land in what was called the Western Territory, that area bounded by the Great Lakes to the north, the Appalachians to the east, the Florida panhandle to the south, and the Mississippi River to the west. Seven states— Massachusetts, Connecticut, New York, Virginia, North Carolina, South Carolina, and Georgia—claimed parts of the territory. Beginning in 1782, one after another state found that managing those lands was a burden, and they turned the land over to Congress. Hoping to raise funds to pay off the war debt, Congress sold large tracts of the lands to speculators. But the value of the land did not rise as it should have. Americans who had already moved into the territory were stymied by the Spanish, who controlled the Mississippi River. The settlers found it easier to move their produce by water, down the Mississippi and then to the eastern seaboard, rather than overland, across the mountains. But the practicality of that route was offset by the high taxes and tariffs Spain collected on the Mississippi. Increased settlement could not begin in earnest without military forces to subdue the Indians and government officials to oversee that settlement in an orderly fashion. The Confederation Congress could provide neither.

The states had their own problems. The state legislatures had also incurred war debts through the sale of bonds. Heavily taxed and, further, reeling under the effects of the weak postwar economy, their citizens pressed for relief. Some states allowed debtors to wriggle out of the terms of contracts and suspended the collection of debts and taxes.

Small farmers, in particular, were burdened—some 90 percent of the American population earned their livelihood from small farms.[3] They wanted their states to issue paper money. Without any monetary value, this money would nonetheless enable them to sell their crops and pay off their debts. Seven compliant states were awash in a sea of their own paper money. Lenders were unwilling to lend, merchants were unwilling to sell, if they must receive payment in depreciated money. Rhode Island printed so much worthless paper money that it was creditors who fled debtors. The state legislature, firmly controlled by small farmers, or agrarians, passed a law requiring that creditors accept paper money.

The states were often bickering among themselves. So powerful was each state's instinct to protect its citizens that courts tended to stand by their own people, putting off legal proceedings or ruling in their favor, when they were sued by citizens of other states. Many states set up high tariffs on goods coming into, or even through, their states. Called imposts, these tariffs were especially handy for New York. The state found that it could avoid taxing its citizens but still raise money by fixing imposts on foreign goods destined for other states but unloaded in New York. The state also put imposts on goods from other states, including firewood from Connecticut and produce from New Jersey that was sold in

New York City. Furious businessmen in Connecticut retaliated by agreeing not to send any goods to all of New York for a year. The New Jersey legislature got back by laying a heavy tax on a lighthouse New York operated on Sandy Hook, part of New Jersey.

Maryland and Virginia were also at loggerheads about navigation rights on the Potomac and Pocomoke rivers and in Chesapeake Bay. To see if they could iron out their differences, representatives from both states met at Mount Vernon in 1785. George Washington was happy to host such a meeting at his home. The Confederation's woes dismayed him. But he also had invested in the Western Territory, and he knew that agreement on navigation rights was essential to the opening—and increase in value—of new land.

That meeting, a success in its own right, provided the impetus for the Annapolis Convention. Scheduled for September 1786, it was designed to bring together all the states to resolve general commercial problems. But only five states sent delegates, among them Alexander Hamilton of New York, John Dickinson of Delaware, and James Madison of Virginia. They recognized that with so few states represented, there was no point in trying to draw up an agreement for commerce throughout the states. Despairing of the Confederation's impotence in every aspect, the delegates recommended to Congress that delegates from all the states convene in Philadelphia on the second Monday in May 1787 "to devise such further provisions as shall appear to them necessary to render the Constitution of the Fœderal Government adequate to the exigencies of the Union."[4]

In Congress, the recommendation gathered dust; it was referred to a committee, but members of the committee were never appointed. Most likely nothing would have happened had it not been for the outbreak of fighting within a state.

Late in 1786, Massachusetts was the scene of Shays's Rebellion. The state's heavy taxes were particularly onerous for farmers already deep in debt. Unable to pay their taxes, farmers saw the courts settle the many lawsuits by confiscating land and imprisoning debtors. A sharp sense of social class against social class led them to conclude that wealthy businessmen in eastern Massachusetts could acquire their land cheaply while farmers lost their livelihood. Led by Daniel Shays, who had served as a captain in the Revolution, irate farmers from western Massachusetts marched on Worcester to stop the state's supreme court session on December 5. They did the same in Springfield on Christmas Day. In late January 1787, the rebels were routed in Springfield, where they hoped to capture weapons in an arsenal there.

The violence alarmed citizens throughout the states. Citizens of other states could not dismiss the uprising as Massachusetts's problem, for every state had its own volatile citizens. For Southerners, it was not difficult to imagine their slaves revolting in a similar fashion. How would they handle such a problem? Congress was in no position to help quell an uprising. John Jay, who had negotiated the Treaty of Paris, was but one of many concerned that Americans had lost sight of their destiny. He sensed that law-abiding citizens were so fearful of anarchy that they would willingly accept a king, even a dictator, just for the assurance of civil order.

Shays's Rebellion was the proverbial straw that broke the camel's back. Holders of war bonds, land speculators, manufacturers, merchants, creditors, hopeful settlers—those Americans had already been prepared to take the risks of a vigorous central government so that they could get on with their lives. The troubles in Massachusetts made others wonder if the risks might not be worth it after all. On February 21, 1787, having resurrected the recommendation from the

Annapolis Convention, Congress cautiously called for a convention "for the sole and express purpose of revising the Articles of Confederation."[5] Each state legislature was invited to send delegates to discuss ways in which the Confederation could be altered so as to make it work. Fifty-five delegates would participate for part or all of the convention that would meet in Philadelphia during the summer of 1787. Of those fifty-five, a vast majority would agree that the Articles of Confederation could not be revised and that the Confederation must, in fact, be scrapped and a nation created in its place.

# 2
# THE CONVENTION OPENS

On Sunday, May 13, 1787, George Washington, escorted by the city troop of Philadelphia and three generals, two colonels, and two majors who had served under him during the Revolution, rode into Philadelphia. The city greeted Washington's arrival with a fanfare of church bells and artillery salutes. The largest and most sophisticated city in all of the states, Philadelphia was pleased to host the Federal Convention, which was to open the next day. Now called Independence Hall, the Pennsylvania State House, where the meetings to revamp the Articles of Confederation would be held, had been the stage for many momentous meetings. The Pennsylvania assembly met there regularly, the Continental Congress had met there, the Declaration of Independence had been signed there, and the Confederation Congress had met there before moving to New York.

Regarded as the states' preeminent citizen, George Washington would be in illustrious company. Avidly interested in the Federal Convention, Thomas Jefferson, then in Paris as minister to France, read the roster of delegates and termed it "an assembly of demi-gods."[1] Many were quite young; nonetheless, they had already distinguished themselves— as signers of the Declaration of Independence, as soldiers in the Revolution, as members of the Continental and Con-

*A session of the Federal Convention, with George Washington presiding (The Bettmann Archive)*

federation congresses, and as state legislators and governors.

As it turned out, the convention could not begin on the appointed day, May 14, because only two states—Pennsylvania and Virginia—had delegates in Philadelphia at the time. Not until May 25 was a quorum reached. New Hampshire would be unrepresented for much of the convention as the state legislature did not name its delegates until June. Rhode Island, then controlled by agrarians, was unrepresented throughout. Enjoying—and profiting from—their power, the legislators of that state were not in the least interested in seeing the Confederation strengthened. (They did not represent the views of all of their constituents; thirteen merchants in Providence, distraught that their state was not taking part, sent a letter to the delegates at the Federal Convention wishing them well in the work before them and expressing their hope that the state's absence would not affect Rhode Island's commercial dealings with the other states.)

When the convention finally got underway, the first order of business was the election of a president to chair the convention. Nominated by Robert Morris of Pennsylvania, George Washington was unanimously elected. Escorted by Morris and John Rutledge of South Carolina, Washington moved to the dais and took the president's chair, decorated with a carved and gilded half-sun rising—or setting—on the top of the chair's high back.

William Jackson, who was not a delegate but was elected as the convention's secretary, then read the credentials sent by all nine states with delegations in attendance that first day. The credentials summarized what delegates might do on behalf of the states they represented. All of the credentials were quite clear that the delegates were sent to the convention to adjust the Articles of Confederation so that the Confederation could function properly.

The delegates next appointed Alexander Hamilton of New York, George Wythe of Virginia, and Charles Pinckney of South Carolina to draw up rules for the convention's proceedings.

At the next meeting, on Monday, May 28, Benjamin Franklin attended for the first time. Then eighty-one years old, he was in such poor health that he got about town in a sedan chair, acquired while he was in Paris, carried by prisoners from the Walnut Street jail. Age had not, however, diminished his zest and mental acuity. President of Pennsylvania, a resident of Philadelphia, learned and still eager to learn, Franklin would frequently entertain the delegates over the course of that long, unusually hot Philadelphia summer. He would devise compromises and, no less important, often provide the anecdote or observation that brought much-needed release in the more argumentative moments.

The rules committee presented its report, which considered every aspect of the convention, from the formalities by which the delegates were to adjourn at the end of the day to the method of recording votes. As finally adopted, several rules were to prove of particular value. First, a vote on any issue did not prevent the delegates from returning to that issue again—and yet again. Rufus King of Massachusetts suggested that votes be recorded by state, not by delegate. As it was, each state, not each delegate, had one vote. It was King's view, however, that recording only delegation votes would make it easier for individual delegates to reconsider and change their position. In addition, a secrecy rule was adopted. Delegates were not to discuss the proceedings with anyone other than fellow delegates; nor could they copy notes from the daily journal without permission. Sentries were placed at the state house doors and outside by the windows of the room where the meetings were taking place so that passersby could not linger there to eavesdrop.

The Virginia delegates had not been at a loss for what to do during the nearly two weeks they were in Philadelphia before the convention finally opened. They had discussed the powers that the Confederation government ought to have and organized them into fifteen resolves. On Tuesday, May 29, Edmund Randolph, governor of Virginia, took the floor to present the delegation's proposals.

The Virginia Plan, as it came to be known, was a group effort, but James Madison's imprint is clearly there. A student of political theory, Madison believed that citizens are often abused by their governments when there is no restraint on the majority's power. To protect against such abuses, power must be limited. Further, that limited power must be divided, with centers of power set one against the other—balanced and checked. The delegates would spend the summer trying to determine the proper limits for government, the equilibrium for the centers of power. An especially active participant in the debates, Madison was at the same time compiling what would prove the most complete record of the proceedings, which was not published until 1840:

> I chose a seat in front of the presiding member with the other members, on my right & left hand. In this favorable position for hearing all that passed, I noted in terms legible & in abbreviations & marks intelligible to myself what was read from the Chair or spoken by the members. . . . I was not absent a single day, nor more than a casual fraction of an hour in any day, so that I could not have lost a single speech, unless a very short one.[2]

Not surprisingly, Madison is often referred to as the father of the Constitution.

The Virginia Plan went far beyond adjusting the Articles of Confederation. There were to be three branches—legislative, executive, and judicial. The legislature would be composed of two branches, both with voting power in proportion to a state's share of the government's expenses or the state's population. The first branch of the legislature would be elected by the people; the second branch of the legislature would be elected by the members of the first branch.

The Virginia Plan did not envision that the states would cease to exist. They would continue to govern on matters that concerned them and their citizens. But the national legislature would be granted greater power than the Confederation Congress had, and it could negative—that is, veto—state laws not in the interest of the United States as a whole. With that and a resolve that members of state governments take an oath to support the national government, the states would clearly lose a measure of their sovereignty.

The executive branch, appointed by the legislative branch, would carry out the legislative branch's acts. In addition, the executive would, with members of the judicial branch, form a council of revision to scrutinize acts passed by the national legislature, as well as acts passed by state legislatures that the national legislature proposed to negative. The council of revision could reject acts passed by the national legislature and its negatives on state legislation. But the Virginia Plan provided a mechanism by which an extraordinary majority of the national legislature could override decisions by the council.

The judicial branch, made up of a supreme tribunal, or court, and inferior tribunals, was to be chosen by the legislative branch. Unlike members of the legislative and executive branches, members of the judicial branch would not serve for limited terms. Jurisdiction—that is, the power to hear certain kinds of cases—was sketched. All of those cases would be heard first by the inferior tribunals. The supreme tribunal would hear appeals.

The plan called for the national government to oversee the admission of new states, and it guaranteed all states, old and new, a republican form of government. The plan also called for provisions for amending the so-called articles of union, even if the legislature did not support the proposed amendments.

Finally, the Virginia Plan proposed that the people of the states, not the state legislatures, ratify whatever plan for the national government was finally drafted. This, too, was an attack on state sovereignty.

Many delegates were instinctively opposed to such a plan. Still, they voted to form a committee of the whole house, chaired by Nathaniel Gorham of Massachusetts, to consider the resolves. Edmund Randolph immediately proposed a revision of the first one. He asserted that the Confederation could never bind the states together. Instead, "a national government ought to be established consisting of a supreme legislative, judiciary and executive."[3]

Supreme? The word took the delegates' breath away. What would happen to the states? Edmund Randolph explained that only certain powers would be turned over to the national government by the states. Gouverneur Morris of Pennsylvania spoke of a national government that would assert its supremacy only where it and the states were in conflict. George Mason of Virginia pointed out that a national government would have to go to war against a state to assert its supremacy. James Wilson of Pennsylvania observed that states have no reality; government can act only on people, not on states.

The delegates were in fact groping for a government that was stronger than a confederation of sovereign states and weaker than a unitary—that is, single—government. Federal governments, in which the central government and the local governments have their own separate spheres of sovereignty, had existed—ancient Greece used such an arrangement—but never had a federal government embraced such a large and diverse area.

Debating each issue, the delegates explored the idea. By June 14, the committee of the whole house had reworked the Virginia Plan. Some of the resolves had been deleted, others agreed to, still others put off for later consideration. With deletions and recastings, the fifteen resolves had grown to nineteen. The delegates had decided that terms for the first branch of the national legislature should be three years, while those for the second branch should be seven. Members of the second branch would be elected by their state legislatures, which were in a better position to know which citizens would make good representatives. Further, the state legislatures' role might increase their support for the government proposed by the convention. In both branches of the national legislature, the number of voting representatives from each state would be determined according to the state's free population plus three-fifths of the slave population to reflect wealth. (The three-fifths formula was not new. In 1783, the Confederation Congress had proposed to the states that it be used for determining contributions owed by the states for the Confederation's expenses.)

The question of suffrage, or voting, in the legislative branch had provoked—and would provoke again—the most contentious debates. Delaware's delegates pointed out that their credentials explicitly forbade them from even discussing a change in voting rules. David Brearley of New Jersey saw redrawing state lines to make equal divisions as the only solution. Others reminded the delegates that their mission was to *revise* the Articles of Confederation. Roger Sherman of Connecticut proposed proportional representation in the first branch, equal representation in the second. Franklin threw his weight, along with an anecdote, to proportional representation in both branches of the legislature.

The executive branch was to consist of one person, who

would hold the position for no more than one term of seven years. The executive himself could negative state and national legislation. Still, that negative could be overridden by a two-thirds vote in both branches of the legislature. The delegates were not prepared to call for inferior tribunals, but left that prerogative to the national legislature to use as needed. The delegates also deleted the suggestion that the articles of union could be amended without the consent of the national legislature.

That same day, June 14, William Paterson of New Jersey rose to say that some delegations wished to propose another plan. Might they have a day to prepare? The convention agreed to adjourn for a day.

The New Jersey Plan, as it was called, proposed a revision of the Articles of Confederation. Taking into account the failures of the Confederation, the New Jersey Plan would give the Confederation Congress authority to impose taxes on imports and on stamps as a way to raise money and to regulate commerce among the states and with foreign countries. Force could be used to make a state comply, but only with the consent of an extraordinary majority of the states. The plan proposed an executive branch consisting of more than one person and a supreme tribunal with limited jurisdiction. The plan accepted the idea of determining state contributions for the Confederation on the basis of population, but it gave no ground to proportional voting in Congress.

The New Jersey Plan was the product of the small states, which feared being overrun by the large states—Massachusetts, Pennsylvania, Virginia. New York was then the fourth-largest state and expected to outstrip the others before long. Nonetheless, it favored a weak national government; with New York raking in so much money through its imposts, Governor George Clinton and the legislature believed that the state would lose more than it would gain from a strong national government. John Lansing of New York discussed the advantages of the New Jersey Plan: the convention had been authorized only to revise the Articles of Confederation, not to pitch it entirely; further, the states would never agree to a government constructed along the lines of the Virginia Plan. But Lansing was skirting the real point—the small states would not give up the equal voting power they had in Congress.

After the New Jersey Plan had been presented, Alexander Hamilton, the one New York delegate out of sympathy with the attitudes of his state, spoke before the convention for an entire day, presenting his view of the ideal government for the states. To his mind, even the Virginia Plan was inadequate. A single executive appointed for life by electors and having the power of the negative; representatives in an upper legislative branch chosen for life; representatives in a lower branch elected by the citizenry for three-year terms; state governors appointed by the national government; all in all, he urged a single, unitary government. The people, Hamilton had concluded, "begin to be tired of an excess of democracy—and what even is the Virginia plan, but pork still, with a little change of the sauce?"[4] Hamilton's proposal, radical even in the eyes of those who favored a strong national government, drew no rebuttal or even discussion.

On Tuesday, June 19, James Madison drew the delegates back to the two plans before them. He went through the New Jersey Plan, raising criticism after criticism. The plan did nothing to smooth dealings among the states. It offered states no help for local disturbances like Shays's Rebellion, which Massachusetts had had difficulty putting down. The plan provided no means by which to hold the states together in a union. Madison then cautioned the small states that by clinging to an unworkable plan, they might impede the adoption of *any* plan. If the Confederation came apart, would they then be safer from abuse at the hands of larger, stronger states? If the states formed regional confederacies, would they be able to enter on any better terms than those proposed in the Virginia Plan? Rufus King called for a vote. By seven to three, with Maryland's delegation divided, the convention returned to the Virginia Plan. But on every question, the dissenters would work to bring the plan closer to the system used for the Confederation.

The delegates began with the legislature. Should it have two branches? The delegates, John Lansing reiterated, were moving far from the organization of the Confederation, which had a single-branch legislature. But the idea of a two-branch legislature was not foreign. England operated with its two houses of Parliament, and all of the states but Pennsylvania and Georgia had two-branch legislatures. Would there be salaries for congressmen, and if so, paid by whom? Benjamin Franklin was opposed to paying anyone in government service. They should serve out of patriotism. But James Madison's experience was that government jobs offering no remuneration were hard to fill. He urged that salaries be paid by the national treasury—state legislatures were notoriously stingy with the delegates they sent to the Confederation Congress—but let the new government's constitution, not the legislators, set the salaries. Should legislators be permitted to hold other government positions? Many at that time did. To the argument that talent should be used as extensively as possible, others pointed to the corruption that that practice had brought about in the English government. How long should terms for the first branch be? Some delegates were adamant that the people be able to scrutinize the work of their representatives every year at the polls.

As for the second branch, that body must have a measure of independence if it was to provide stability, so James Madison pushed for nine-year terms. Nathaniel Gorham proposed six-year terms, with a third of the Senate terms ending every two years. Who would elect members of the second branch? On what was representation to be based—property assessments, as was designated by the Articles of Confederation, or population, as had been suggested by the Confederation Congress in 1783?

All of these questions sparked heated debate, but every delegate knew that they were circling the single most important question—that of proportional versus equal representation. It could not be postponed forever. On June 27, Luther Martin, the longwinded, argumentative delegate from Maryland whose name lives still for his harangues in the Federal Convention, spoke for three hours, then "He was much too exhausted he said to finish his remarks, and reminded the House that he should tomorrow, resume them."[5] He insisted that the powers of the national government be kept confined; that the purpose of the national government was to assist state governments, not to consume them; that the states, not the people, should approve the plan for the national government, for the people had already delegated that authority to their state governments; that equal representation among the states was the basic principle of a confederation—just as individuals have an equal vote in their states, so too should the states have an equal vote in the national government. Martin asserted that the Virginia Plan, with proportional representation, would never be accepted. He was unmoved by the soothing words that all the states shared the same interests, that large states would do nothing to destroy the small states. If that were so, he challenged, why were the large states so insistent on proportional representation?

Tedious though he was, Luther Martin gave vent to the fears of small states. James Madison offered reassurances, pointing out that proportional representation was already in use within the states, with larger counties having more representatives than smaller counties. Gunning Bedford of Delaware said that the small states would ally with a foreign power before giving up equal voting—no idle threat.

Benjamin Franklin was distressed by the lack of agreement and wondered if it wasn't time to call upon the Almighty for guidance. He suggested that the clergy be asked to come each morning to offer prayers. Some delegates worried about public reaction. What would Philadelphians think if, in the middle of the convention, clergy were to start appearing regularly? One legend grew up that Alexander Hamilton sneered at this suggestion of a need for such "foreign aid."[6] The question was academic, Hugh Williamson of North Carolina pointed out. There were no funds to pay a chaplain.

The fierce wrangle over representation continued. William Samuel Johnson of Connecticut renewed Roger Sherman's suggestion of a compromise allowing both kinds of representation. Committed to proportional representation, James Madison repeated that if small states did not join with the others, all the states might find themselves completely alone or at the mercy of regional confederacies. Alexander Hamilton extended that point to suggest that states on their own or small confederacies of states would invite alliances with foreign powers, threatening their neighbors.

James Madison believed that states divided not according to size but according to whether they had slaves, and he saw in this the possibility of a compromise. Perhaps one branch of the legislature might have voting based on the number of free inhabitants; the other, voting based on the number of free inhabitants and slaves. "By this arrangement the Southern Scale would have the advantage in one House, and the Northern in the other,"[7] he reasoned.

Benjamin Franklin, returning to the dilemma in terms of

size, noted that those states favoring equal representation feared the loss of their liberties, while those favoring proportional representation resented the idea of paying more for the maintenance of the government without having a corresponding say in its decisions. Building on Roger Sherman's proposal for equal *and* proportional representation, he suggested that states have equal representation in the second branch but that, in money matters, voting in that branch should be proportional.

In a vote on equal representation in the second branch on July 2, the outcome was a tie, with Georgia's delegation divided. The convention had come to a standstill, and the delegates knew it. A committee of one delegate from each state was established to spend the next day and the Fourth of July to find some compromise about representation. If a satisfactory compromise could not be found, the convention would have to be dissolved.

# 3

# A RISING SUN

Reconvening on the fifth of July, the Federal Convention heard the report of the committee charged with finding a solution to the problem of legislative representation. Even the committee members were unhappy with their results. In addition to the compromises proposed earlier by Roger Sherman and Benjamin Franklin, the committee had considered yet another suggestion from Sherman—that states have equal votes in the second branch of the legislature but that no measure would pass unless states voting for it represented a majority of the population of all the states taken together. The committee had finally agreed to recommend Sherman's original proposal with a new twist suggested by Franklin: the second branch would have equal representation while the first branch would have proportional representation—one representative for every forty thousand inhabitants, including three-fifths of the slave population; all bills concerning money must be proposed in the first branch; the second branch would vote for or against those bills only as presented.

The delegates did not immediately accept the committee's recommendation. Supporters of proportional representation continued to feel that a basic principle was being denied, but they began to show signs of resignation. "If we do not

The signature page from the Constitution of the United States
(The National Archives)

come to some agreement among ourselves some foreign sword will probably do the work for us,"[1] Elbridge Gerry of Massachusetts allowed. Gouverneur Morris and John Rutledge expressed doubts about representation by population. After all, a prime purpose of government was to protect property. It was moved that taxation then be tied to representation. Slaves were at that time regarded as property. South Carolina and Georgia were willing to pay taxes on all of their slaves, but the other slave states were not. When Edmund Randolph proposed that they return to representation based only on population, many were anxious about the future, when the Western Territory would bloom into full-fledged states. What might the rough westerners do when they became a majority? Gerry proposed that no new states ever be allowed more representation than the original thirteen. Again it was moved that representation be proportional in both branches.

Having haggled over every aspect of representation, the delegates took a vote on July 16 on the committee's original recommendation. Connecticut, New Jersey, Delaware, Maryland, and North Carolina voted aye; Pennsylvania, Virginia, South Carolina, and Georgia voted nay; Massachusetts was divided. No delegates from New York were present; Alexander Hamilton would return, but John Lansing and Richard Yates, having departed on July 10 in disgust, would not. Edmund Randolph proposed adjourning so that all might consider their positions. William Paterson agreed that adjourning sine die—that is, without plans to reconvene—was a good idea. Aghast, Randolph retorted that he had meant only that they adjourn until the next day to allow the delegates to reflect on this impasse. The convention agreed to reconvene the next day. Early that morning, before the day's session began, some of the delegates gathered to discuss the options. There, delegates from the large states concluded that the small states would never yield on the issue of equal representation in the second branch. The large states could no longer oppose them.

Called the Great Compromise or the Connecticut Compromise, the agreement to use proportional representation in the first branch of the legislature and equal representation in the second branch ended the impasse that had consumed some six weeks. In addition to keeping the convention—and the states—together, the compromise provided the basis for our federal system, which is neither as loose as a confederation nor as tight as a unitary government. Yet another two months would be needed to work out the myriad details of the Constitution, but lines of battle were not to be drawn so firmly ever again.

Turning to the sphere of the legislature's attention, the delegates chose to give it power "to legislate in all cases for the general interests of the Union, and also in those to which the States are separately incompetent, or in which the harmony of the United States may be interrupted by the exercise of individual legislation." They then changed their mind about the power to negate state legislation; the national legislature would not have that power. However, they agreed to a motion put forward by Luther Martin that legislative acts and treatises of the national government take precedence. Judges in state courts would be bound first to national law, then to state law. Here are the roots of what was to be called the Supremacy Clause; the national government would come first, and was thus supreme.

Sketching in the second legislative branch more fully, the delegates debated the number of members. Too many members would be expensive. Further, too many could not function as a truly deliberative body. Two for each state was agreed to unanimously. Breaking from the system used by the Confederation Congress, the convention decided that each member, not each state delegation, would have a vote. If a state's members divided on an issue, the state's voting power was a wash. The convention's accord on this point indicates the harmony achieved by the Great Compromise: only Maryland opposed it.

Discussion of the executive followed. It was decided that executive power would be vested in one person, selected by the national legislature for a term of seven years. He was to be eligible for another term. A few days later, the term was revised to six years. The delegates went back and forth on who would elect the executive—state legislatures or the national legislature. If he was elected by the national legislature but was to remain independent, he could not be eligible for reelection. In that case the executive might have a longer term—terms of eight to twenty years were discussed. The convention settled on the original proposal outlined in the Virginia Plan: a single term of seven years; election by the national legislature.

The Virginia Plan envisioned a judiciary composed of a supreme tribunal and inferior tribunals as needed. Some delegates disliked the idea of federal courts sitting in the states. So the convention voted to leave the question of inferior tribunals to the legislature, give judicial appointment power to the second branch, and paint jurisdiction with a broad brush.

How the Constitution should be approved was once again debated. Article XIII of the Articles of Confederation required unanimous approval by the state legislatures for any alteration of the articles, and the congressional resolution calling for the Federal Convention specified that the delegates' proposals would be treated in that manner. But Edmund Randolph insisted that state legislators, whose powers would wane under a strong national government, would oppose the Constitution for their own personal reasons; ratification must be by conventions of the citizenry. Elbridge Gerry thought that no consensus would emerge from such conventions. James Madison put the issue in theoretical terms: it was not appropriate for the state legislatures to pass judgment on a national government that, if approved, would be supreme to the state governments. Further, while the Articles of Confederation derived its powers from the states, the proposed constitution derived its powers from the people. Thus the people must ratify. Madison's view was intellectually consistent. Still, it is clear that if the Constitution stood any chance of adoption, it was with the citizens, not the state legislators.

The convention had again worked its way through all the resolutions of the Virginia Plan. On July 26, John Rutledge, Edmund Randolph, Nathaniel Gorham, Oliver Ellsworth, and James Wilson were elected to a Committee of Detail charged with organizing all of the convention's decisions and drawing up the first draft of the Constitution. For the next ten days, while the Committee of Detail worked, the other delegates had a respite. George Washington made a journey to Valley Forge, where his troops had somehow endured that harsh winter of 1777–78, then whiled away several days fishing. Some delegates took the opportunity to go home. Others, too far from home to get there and back during the break, stayed in Philadelphia to enjoy the pleasures their work had prevented them from sampling.

Reconvening on August 6, the delegates were given printed copies of the draft prepared by the Committee of Detail. The committee had started with all of the resolutions voted by the convention up to July 23; then wove in some points from a plan proposed by Charles Pinckney, which had not been debated, and the New Jersey Plan; and looked at proposals for strengthening the union offered six years earlier in the Confederation Congress—proposals with which Edmund Randolph and Oliver Ellsworth, having helped prepare them, were familiar. In addition, the Committee of Detail had applied formal names to the various government entities. The executive was referred to as the president, and was to be addressed as "His Excellency." The legislature, or Congress, was composed of the House of Representatives and the Senate. The supreme tribunal had become the Supreme Court. The Committee of Detail had also drafted a preamble to the Constitution. "We the people," it began, "of the States of New Hampshire, Massachusetts, Rhode-Island . . ." listing all thirteen states as they ran north to south. This constitution derived its powers from the people of the states, not the states.

Going through the twenty-three articles of the draft, the delegates agreed that they must reconsider the question of who could vote in national elections. As put forward by the draft, voting would be determined by a state's voting requirements. All of the states set requirements, based on property holdings or tax payments, but each state had its own standards. Many delegates believed that a property requirement was essential—James Madison, for one, thought that the propertyless might one day grow so numerous that, armed with the vote, they could overwhelm the propertied. Benjamin Franklin, the true democrat, believed that the common man was given less credit than he deserved. In the end, property requirements as set forth by the Committee of Detail were left undisturbed: any man who could vote in elections for the more numerous branch of his state's legislature could vote in national elections. However, property qualifications, though proposed, were not set up for congressmen. Franklin observed that "Some of the greatest rogues he was ever acquainted with, were the richest rogues."[2] The provision requiring that all bills concerning money be written by the House of Representatives was redebated and ultimately softened, allowing the Senate to offer amendments to the House's bills.

Sometime in July, a citizen of Connecticut anonymously sent out a circular letter proposing that George III's second son, the Bishop of Osnaburgh, be installed as King of America. Aghast, citizens throughout the states wrote anxiously to the delegates in Philadelphia asking about plans for a monarchy. On August 22 the *Pennsylvania Journal* published a statement issued by the convention: ". . . tho' we cannot, affirmatively, tell you what we are doing, we can, negatively, tell you what we are not doing—we never once thought of a king."[3]

Sensing a fear of a powerful executive, the convention looked again at the presidency. The president must be a native-born citizen and would be referred to simply as "Mr. President." He would serve for four years. After scores of votes taken since June, the delegates decided on a complex electoral system whereby the people would choose the executive. A vice president, elected in the same manner and at the same time, would succeed the president if he were unable to carry out his duties or were removed from office—impeached. Specific executive powers were itemized, but none were prohibited. The president was given the power to nominate federal judges, but the Senate was given the power of final approval—"advice and consent." To check an unwise Congress, the president was given the power to veto legislation; but to check an unwise president, Congress was given the power to override that veto so long as a two-thirds majority in both the House and Senate could be mustered.

The matters on which Congress might legislate were carefully spelled out. Importantly, Congress could lay and collect taxes. The delegates agreed that the new government should assume the debts incurred by the Continental and Confederation congresses. Foreign and interstate trade, so bedeviling for the Confederation, were to be regulated by the national government. Congress might tax imports, but conflict arose on the question of taxing exports. Southern states feared giving taxing power on exports to the national government, where northern states might combine to tax their products mercilessly. States that had to ship through other states feared leaving taxing power on exports to the states. The convention voted that neither the national government nor the states might lay taxes on exports. Congress was also given the power "to make all Laws which shall be necessary and proper for carrying into Execution the foregoing powers, and all other Powers vested by this Constitution in the Government of the United States, or in any Department or Officer thereof." Known as the Necessary and Proper Clause, it gave the government the ability to address unforeseen situations.

Giving Congress extensive powers corrected only one part of the ineffectiveness of the Confederation. For the national government to work, restrictions must be placed on the states. Most emphatically, the states were prohibited from issuing paper money. Nor could they meddle with contracts. Finally, the Constitution and the laws of the United States "shall be the supreme Law of the Land." State judges would be bound first by the national government's laws, then by their states'. State government officials would have to swear to support the Constitution.

The Committee of Detail had drafted a clause that specified that the slave trade be neither prohibited nor taxed. Luther Martin protested. He wished to see the influx of slaves curbed, for if three-fifths of the slave population was to be a part of the formula for representation, states might be encouraged to expand their slave population. In addition to skewing representation, large slave populations might revolt, requiring the national government to go to the aid of a state. Others pointed out the unfairness of exempting only slaves from an import tax. South Carolina and Georgia were the only states that still permitted the importation of slaves— slaves died too quickly there for the states to abandon importation—and they made it clear that taxing imported slaves was one thing, but prohibiting the slave trade was another. Prohibit the slave trade, and South Carolina and Georgia would not join the union. The convention compromised by protecting the slave trade until 1808 and setting the import tax at no more than ten dollars per slave. All delegations went along with a motion that a state must return slaves and indentured servants who had fled other states. For the time being, the institution of slavery would thus be better protected by the Constitution than ever before.

On through the draft the delegates went. They provided for the admission of new states, though they did not specify if new states would be on an equal footing with the original states. They empowered the national government to raise an army for protecting the states from foreign invasion and, at a state's request, internal disorder. They made provision for the site of the national government, allowing Congress to accept land "not exceeding ten Miles square" offered by some state. They saw that there was no check on the power to make treaties, which the Committee of Detail had given to the Senate. It was decided that the president would make treaties "by and with the advice and Consent of the Senate," consent of two-thirds of the senators in attendance.

Knowing that if the Constitution was to endure, it must accommodate new needs and different times, they provided for its amendment. Two-thirds of each house of Congress or two-thirds of the states, through their legislatures, were needed for an amendment to be proposed. Acceptance by three-fourths of the states, either by the legislature or by a special convention, was needed for it to be ratified.

Again the delegates considered how this constitution was

to be ratified. Any method other than the one provided for by the Articles of Confederation was technically illegal—a point pressed by Luther Martin and Daniel Carroll, also of Maryland. But all the other delegations agreed to ratification by special conventions of the people. Further, they agreed that nine states would be sufficient for the establishment of the national government.

On Saturday September 8, a Committee of Style and Arrangement, composed of Rufus King, William Samuel Johnson, Alexander Hamilton, Gouverneur Morris, and James Madison, was appointed to polish the draft that the delegates had reviewed and revised. The following Wednesday, the committee presented its handiwork. It had condensed the twenty-three articles of the draft prepared by the Committee of Detail into seven. The Preamble was significantly altered: "We the people of the States of . . ." had been changed to "We the People of the United States. . . ." The committee reasoned that the new government could be set up as soon as nine states had ratified; no one knowing which states would be the first to ratify or even if all the states would eventually ratify, the phrasing of the first draft was inappropriate. But beyond the question of correctness, the change emphasized that the new government derived its powers from and operated on the people, not the states. (Later, those who opposed ratification would point to the Preamble as proof that the national government would engulf the state governments.) The committee had also drafted a covering letter to Congress, explaining why the delegates had written a constitution rather than revise the Articles of Confederation. The manner in which the Constitution was to be ratified, originally part of the text of the document itself, was cast as a separate resolution of the convention.

The tempo of the last few days was very fast. The Pennsylvania assembly was in session and needed its meeting room, and the delegates to the convention, some having been in Philadelphia for four months, were anxious to conclude their work. Proposed changes were handled with dispatch. George Mason proposed that a bill of rights—a statement of individual liberties that the government could not violate—be included in the Constitution. For a host of reasons, a bill of rights was seen as unnecessary. Mason's proposal was voted down unanimously.

On Saturday, September 15, Edmund Randolph rose to announce that he could not sign the Constitution. While he agreed that the Confederation had powerful defects, he was unhappy with "the indefinite and dangerous powers given by the Constitution to Congress."[4] He urged the delegates to take up George Mason's suggestion, advanced a few weeks earlier, that state conventions be set up to look at the proposed constitution and offer their views, to be considered by a second federal convention.

George Mason then took the floor. He deplored the haste with which the convention had concluded its work. He believed that the document had many flaws, but he would sign the Constitution—only if there were some mechanism by which the people could call for alterations before being asked to ratify it.

Elbridge Gerry, too, had complaints—eleven, to be precise. They ranged from "the duration and re-eligibility of the Senate" to "the general power of the Legislature to make what laws they may please to call necessary and proper."[5] A second convention must be held.

Edmund Randolph's motion for a second general convention was voted down by every state delegation, and the Constitution as amended was agreed to unanimously. The document was sent out to be engrossed—that is, copied out in fine script. Five hundred printed copies were also ordered.

On Monday, September 17, William Jackson, the secretary, read the engrossed Constitution. Benjamin Franklin had prepared a speech, which he gave to James Wilson to read for him. The Constitution, Franklin believed, was not perfect, but perhaps he would change his mind—he had often found that his first opinions were incorrect. He went on:

> . . . I agree to this Constitution with all its faults, if they are such . . . I doubt too whether any other Convention we can obtain may be able to make a better Constitution. For when you assemble a number of men to have the advantage of their joint wisdom, you inevitably assemble with those men, all their prejudices, their passions, their errors of opinion, their local interests, and their selfish views. From such an Assembly can a perfect production be expected? It therefore astonishes me, Sir, to find this system approaching so near to perfection as it does; and I think it will astonish our enemies, who are waiting with confidence to hear that our councils are confounded like those of the Builders of Babel; and that our States are on the point of separation, only to meet hereafter for the purpose of cutting one another's throats. Thus I consent, Sir, to this Constitution because I expect no better, and because I am not sure, that it is not the best.[6]

When James Wilson finished reading Benjamin Franklin's speech, Franklin himself moved that the Constitution be signed. Nathaniel Gorham asked that the delegates consider changing the ratio of representation from one for every forty thousand citizens to one for every thirty thousand. George Washington, who throughout the convention had spoken only in his capacity as president of the convention, hoped the delegates would not think it improper if in this one case he offered his own views. He urged that they agree to the change, for he too believed that the representation as set was inadequate, and he wished there to be as few causes as possible for the people to reject their work. Gorham's motion passed unanimously.

Before the delegates could return to Benjamin Franklin's motion that they sign, Edmund Randolph again took the floor. Franklin's speech had clearly made an impression. Randolph restated his position: though he would not sign, he would not necessarily oppose the Constitution during the ratification period. What was clear, though unsaid, was that Randolph would not saddle himself with a position that might later prove a political liability. He was not sure that nine states would ratify, and he did not want to end up on the losing side.

For his part, Gouverneur Morris declared, he thought the plan before them was the best that could be achieved. He reminded the delegates that they would sign the document in the name of their states; the states would be unanimous although the delegates would not. Alexander Hamilton urged that every delegate sign. Richard Yates and John Lansing having quit in July, Hamilton could not sign for his state, but he could, and would, sign for himself.

Hugh Williamson suggested that the delegates sign the letter to Congress, not the Constitution. William Blount, also of North Carolina, said that he would not sign the Constitution but that he would sign the letter stating that the document was the unanimous agreement of the states in attendance. Once again, Benjamin Franklin offered a compromise. He proposed that they sign the Constitution itself under the notation "Done in Convention by the Unanimous Consent of the States present. . . ." And that is how it was signed.

Of the delegates present that day, Elbridge Gerry, George Mason, and Edmund Randolph did not sign the Constitution. George Washington and the thirty-seven other delegates in attendance signed, with George Read signing for

John Dickinson, who was ill at home in Delaware but had sent a letter authorizing his signature. Unsure of how the people would respond to their work, unsure if their blueprint would give rise to a sound government, they signed by state, running north to south. It was Benjamin Franklin, the old, wise optimist, who offered the most eloquent assurance: "Whilst the last members were signing it," James Madison wrote in his notes,

> Doctr. Franklin looking towards the Presidents Chair, at the back of which a rising sun happened to be painted, observed to a few members near him, that Painters had found it difficult to distinguish in their art a rising from a setting sun. I have, said he, often and often in the course of the Session, and the vicissitudes of my hopes and fears as to its issue, looked at that behind the President without being able to tell whether it was rising or setting: But now at length I have the happiness to know that it is a rising and not a setting Sun.[7]

# 4

# THE RATIFICATION CONVENTIONS

Those delegates to the Federal Convention who had labored through that oppressively hot Philadelphia summer of 1787 immediately dispersed, not to rest but to work for or against ratification. James Madison, Nathaniel Gorham, and Rufus King, members of the Confederation Congress, hurried to New York, where the Congress was in session. They would do what they could to mollify members of Congress who disapproved of what the delegates to the Federal Convention had done. George Washington went home to Mount Vernon, where he would carry on a correspondence with the Constitution's supporters and opponents alike. George Mason set to work on *Objections to the Constitution*, published in October. Setting aside his own disappointment in the Constitution, Alexander Hamilton would devote himself to winning the ratification battle in New York. Hamilton knew that New York would most likely not ratify, but he began outlining the topics to be covered in the series of eighty-five essays called *The Federalist*. Written under the pen name Publius by Hamilton, Madison, and John Jay, they were published in New York papers beginning on October 27, 1787. And although they were addressed to New Yorkers, the essays found an avid readership throughout the states. *The Federalist* was essentially campaign literature, but it

One of a series of eleven editorial cartoons published in the
Massachusetts Centinel *chronicling the progress of ratification of
the Constitution (Library of Congress)*

was—and remains—a brilliant, comprehensive explanation and defense of the Constitution.

Once the proposed constitution was made public, people began taking sides. There were the Federalists, those who believed that the weaknesses of the Confederation would soon bring the demise of the Confederation and then of the states themselves. Seeing a strong national government as the only way to unleash the American potential, they set out to win support for the Constitution—for a nation. On the other side were the Antifederalists, who were convinced that a strong national government would annihilate first the states, with their diverse economies and interests, then the individual. The American Revolution was fresh in their mind. Why sacrifice so much to throw off one oppressive central government, then put another in its place?

In general, opposition to the proposed national government was strongest among small farmers and debtors advocating paper-money schemes. Above and beyond the powers given to the national government, they were apt to regard the Constitution as a format for an aristocracy; look, they said, at the procedures for selecting senators, the president, and members of the judiciary. But Mason's primary criticism of the Constitution—the lack of a bill of rights—concerned many other citizens. To the reply that many states had bills of rights that afforded citizens all the protections they needed, Mason countered that no state's bill of rights offered any protection when set against the Constitution's Supremacy Clause. Mason was correct. Try as they might, Federalists could not overcome this essential flaw in the Constitution.

In Pennsylvania, the Federalists pressed for early ratification. The faster the process, the greater the difficulty for Antifederalists to organize opposition to the Constitution. In addition, Pennsylvania Federalists hoped that their state would have the distinction of being the first to ratify. Earlier congresses had met in Philadelphia; leading the way in ratifying the Constitution might be rewarded by settling the new government there. When the Federal Convention finally adjourned, the Federalist members of the Pennsylvania assembly immediately proposed that a date be set for a ratification convention.

The state's Antifederalist assemblymen seized this opportunity to stall. On September 28, a day before the assembly was to adjourn, they pointed out that the Confederation Congress, then sitting in New York, had not made its views on the Constitution known. (In fact, that very day Congress sent the Constitution to the states with no recommendation, either for or against ratification.) The Federalists insisted that a date for a convention be set that afternoon. Nineteen Antifederalists responded by keeping to their lodgings. As a consequence, the assembly lacked a quorum.

That night, Philadelphia's streets were alive with restive swarms of partisans. The next morning, a mob took care of the problem of a quorum. They broke windows of the lodging house where the Antifederalist assemblymen were staying, seized two, and carried them against their will to the Pennsylvania State House. Spectators in the gallery cheered as a motion to hold a ratifying convention in late November passed. The vote was 45 to 2.

With the decision for or against ratification so close at hand, Pennsylvania's Federalists and Antifederalists scurried to organize and broadcast their arguments. The *Gazetteer* published passionate, sarcastic articles by Antifederalists writing under the pen names Centinel, Plain Truth, and John Humble. James Wilson, regarded by many as the best lawyer among the delegates at the Federal Convention, took the lead in articulating the Federalist position. Throughout the ratifying convention, he explained and defended the document, reassuring the doubters in calm, logical terms that the proposed national government could not oppress them. His thorough, cogent analysis would be taken up by Federalists in all the other states.

The Antifederalists proposed that fifteen amendments be recommended to Congress when Pennsylvania sent in its ratification instrument, but they were outvoted. On December 12, 1787, delegates to Pennsylvania's ratifying convention voted 46 to 23 to accept the Constitution. Irate, the Antifederalists published "The Address and Reasons of Dissent of the Minority of the Convention," an article that included the amendments they had wanted considered. Antifederalist fury with the vote was slow to cool. At a rally in Carlisle a few days after Christmas, James Wilson was beaten by Antifederalists armed with clubs.

As it turned out, Pennsylvania earned the distinction as the most violent in ratification, not as the first. Delaware's delegates voted unanimously to adopt the Constitution on December 7. New Jersey's vote, taken on December 18, was also unanimous. Georgia followed suit on January 2, 1788. A week later, Connecticut ratified by a vote of 128 to 40. Why ratification went so smoothly in these four states is unclear—contemporaneous records offer little information. But Delaware, New Jersey, and Connecticut shipped through other states, and would thus profit from the national government's control of foreign trade. Georgia was anticipating Indian attacks and might need outside help to defend its citizens. All four states would benefit by the Constitution.

Massachusetts's ratification convention opened in Boston on January 9. Federalists throughout the states watched anxiously to see what would happen, for many citizens of Massachusetts were against the Constitution because it did not contain a bill of rights. Further, the Antifederalists there were both prominent and numerous. Samuel Adams, James Winthrop, and James Warren, all of whom had played major roles in the Revolution, were by nature inclined to resist the establishment of a national government. John Hancock, governor of the state and president of the ratification convention, had not taken a position. Some predicted that he would wait for an indication of how the vote would go, then join the winning side. Adams, believing the national government might overpower the state governments, would nonetheless support it if it were amended. Further, he would do what he could to woo Hancock to its cause.

Massachusetts's Federalists frantically cast about for some means by which to gain ratification. In the end, they employed the strategy Pennsylvania Antifederalists had unsuccessfully tried: ratification with recommended amendments. They put together nine amendments for the convention's consideration, and Theophilus Parsons prepared a speech for their presentation. Satisfied that the series of amendments—Adams termed it the Conciliatory Proposition—covered his concerns, Samuel Adams and a delegation of Federalists called on John Hancock. Their courtship was made easy work because of Hancock's vanity and ambition. Hancock was promised important support in his next race for the governorship. More succulent still was the callers' mention of the presidency. Acknowledging that George Washington would no doubt become president if Virginia ratified, they pointed out that Antifederalist sentiment was especially strong in that state. If Virginia did not ratify, thus making Washington ineligible for the presidency, Massachusetts would nominate Hancock for the position. Hancock was captivated.

John Hancock made his first appearance at the ratification convention on January 30. There he delivered the speech written by Theophilus Parsons and presented the Conciliatory Proposition (never suggesting that it was not his own work). Many delegates complained that few of the amendments in the Conciliatory Proposition dealt with individual rights. Samuel Adams submitted additional amendments, which the convention rejected—the records do not indicate why. On February 6, Massachusetts ratified the Constitution by a vote of 187 to 168, then agreed to recommend the Conciliatory Proposition to Congress.

Massachusetts, the sixth state to ratify, was followed by Maryland. Luther Martin, a delegate to the Federal Convention, remained adamantly opposed to the Constitution and strove to convince his state that its liberty would vanish under the proposed government. But Maryland ratified handily, voting 63 to 11 on April 26. During the debate, William Paca had proposed that Maryland follow Massachusetts's example and send recommended amendments to Congress, but the Federalist majority would not even entertain the question. After the vote for ratification, Paca raised his proposal again, and a committee was formed to consider twenty-eight amendments. The committee accepted thirteen. Antifederalists wanted the other fifteen to be heard by the convention as a whole, at which point the Federalists refused to recommend *any* amendments. Frustrated, the Antifederalists published all twenty-eight in a pamphlet.

South Carolina followed on May 23, voting 149 to 73 to ratify. Antifederalists there tried to adjourn the convention for five months, but Federalist sentiment was simply too strong. Still, Antifederalists did succeed in recommending four amendments to Congress.

With South Carolina, only one more state was needed for the Constitution to go into effect. New Hampshire's ratification convention had opened in April. Federalists there had changed the minds of some delegates initially opposed to the Constitution, but many of those delegates believed they could not vote for ratification before discussing the matter with the voters who had sent them to the convention.

The Federalists agreed to adjourn without a vote. In this case, delay might be the winning strategy. They would use the next few months to build the case for ratification, but whether enough votes could be changed was very much in doubt.

While New Hampshire's convention was in adjournment, Virginia's ratification convention opened on June 2. Antifederalist forces there—including such eminent citizens as Patrick Henry, Richard Henry Lee, James Monroe, and George Mason—were excellent debaters, articulate and prepared. Virginia's refusal to ratify would considerably strengthen the hand of Antifederalists in New York and North Carolina, where prospects for ratification already looked dim. Indeed, in New York, the legislature's resolution calling for a convention barely passed, and an effort by state senators to postpone it failed by just one vote. As for Antifederalist sentiment in Rhode Island, why, that state had been against even participating in a revision of the Articles of Confederation. Further, in a referendum held in March 1788, Rhode Islanders had voted against ratification of the Constitution. New Hampshire, Virginia, New York, North Carolina, Rhode Island—if all five states agreed not to ratify, the Confederation would continue.

What no one was able to divine until the Virginia convention got underway was what position Edmund Randolph would take. Randolph urged ratification. Taking the floor, he asserted that the Constitution as it stood was unacceptable. Properly amended, however, it would have his support. Randolph then went on to say that he would have wished for previous amendments—amendments approved by the states before they ratified the Constitution itself. But he pointed out that eight states had already ratified. It was now too late for previous amendments. Subsequent amendments—amendments made after the new government was in place—would have to do.

Patrick Henry rose to challenge Edmund Randolph's integrity. "Something extraordinary must have operated so great a change in his opinions,"[1] Henry suggested darkly. Henry did not have to be explicit. It was a foregone conclusion that George Washington would be the first president if Virginia joined the eight states that had ratified. Was the ambitious Randolph's support rooted in a desire for a position in the new government? That night Henry challenged Randolph to a duel, and, while nothing came of the challenge, it signified the furious passions aroused.

Edmund Randolph's enrollment in the Federalist cause profoundly affected the debate. The question was no longer whether to ratify but whether previous or subsequent amendments would accompany Virginia's assent. Patrick Henry ridiculed the idea of agreeing to a government before knowing the terms of that government. Randolph responded that, eight states having ratified, the issue was whether the states would bind together into one union or proceed as thirteen separate countries. On June 25, Virginia ratified the Constitution, 89 to 79. Henry's Declaration of Rights (comprising twenty articles to be appended to the Constitution), along with twenty subsequent amendments (alterations to the text of the Constitution), were then drafted and agreed to by the convention.

The delegates were at the time unaware that Virginia was not the ninth but the tenth state to ratify; New Hampshire had voted 57 to 46 for ratification, with twelve recommended amendments, on June 21. According to one story, the margin might have been slimmer still. It is said that several Antifederalists were being dined at the home of a Federalist when the vote was taken.

The Fourth of July, 1788, Philadelphia celebrated the ratification by ten states, and thus the establishment, of the Constitution. Two floats—one of the unseaworthy scow *Confederacy*, captained by Imbecility; the other of the solid ship

*Constitution*, ready for the heaviest seas—were moved through the city streets as ebullient Philadelphians cheered. In New York, Governor George Clinton was dismayed; he had heard the news of Virginia's vote only two days earlier. Thinking that Edmund Randolph would oppose the Constitution, Clinton had written his fellow governor proposing that both Virginia and New York demand previous amendments. Randolph had not made the letter public. As leader of the Antifederalists in his state, Clinton recognized that Virginia's decision was a significant setback for him and his followers.

There would be a national government based on the Constitution as it was written, but would New York be a part of it? Federalists could say that New York would suffer without the union, but they knew, too, that the union would suffer without New York. The state was growing quickly and would soon become the largest state. But even if its population had been insignificant, it was still critical. New York City was a principal port, through which other states traded. And without New York, the New England states would be physically cut off from the rest of the nation.

When the New York convention opened on June 17, two-thirds of the delegates had been prepared to vote against ratification. The lack of a bill of rights was deemed but one reason to vote against the document; in the course of the debates, delegates demanded thirty-two amendments. Alexander Hamilton had considered a bill of rights unnecessary and positively dangerous too, but he would accept one. He would also accept amendments—so long as they were subsequent amendments. Antifederalists then insisted on sending a circular letter to all of the states calling for another federal convention to revise the Constitution as adopted. A proposed bill of rights and subsequent amendments, as well as a circular letter to all the states—with these strings attached, enough Antifederalists came over for ratification to pass on July 26. But it was a close call: 30 to 27.

North Carolina's convention opened on July 21 but adjourned sine die on August 2. A vast majority of the delegates were Antifederalists who, spurning the example of other states, would have no part of recommended amendments. By a vote of 184 to 84, the convention chose to postpone its decision until a second federal convention considered the declaration of rights and twenty-six amendments North Carolina had drawn up. Only on November 21, 1789, when the national government was in operation, did the convention vote for ratification. By then, Congress had sent the Bill of Rights to the states that were part of the union. But the political isolation North Carolina felt had proved even more powerful. The strong Antifederalist sentiment there was broken; the vote for ratification was 184 to 77.

Rhode Island, firmly committed to the status quo in 1787, remained so until May 29, 1790. Its convention ratified by a narrow margin—34 to 32—and under duress; the national government had voted to terminate commercial relations with the state, and Rhode Island cities where Federalist opinion was strong had moved to secede from the state and join the national government.

That the Constitution was ratified is as much a marvel as the Constitution itself. The framers had made a novel proposition—that the people permit the establishment of a government above their own state governments. As conceived by the framers, the national government was unlike that of any other nation. For many Americans whose world view extended no farther than the boundaries of their small farms, this Constitution was a worrisome document. Would the awesome national government gobble up their state governments? Would it meddle in every small aspect of their lives? Would it lay heavy taxes on them? Would it take them off to fight in wars against foreign powers? Those Americans were carried along by the ardor of the Federalists, whose world view encompassed the unsettled land to the west and untapped markets in other states and foreign countries. John Marshall, who would become the nation's most important chief justice of the Supreme Court, saw the promise in union. But recognizing the powerful fear of disunion, he observed that "in some of the adopting states a majority of the people were in the opposition. In all of them, the numerous amendments which were proposed demonstrate the reluctance with which the new government was accepted; and that a dread of dismemberment, not an approbation of the particular system under consideration, had induced an acquiescence in it."[2]

# 5

# THE BILL OF RIGHTS

On May 4, 1789, Representative James Madison announced to the House that he would soon offer amendments to the Constitution that would satisfy the demand for a bill of rights. The first Congress was not especially interested. Having been in session for little more than a month, Congress was preoccupied with the myriad decisions that must be made in order to transform the blueprint drawn up by the framers and approved by the people into a strong, solid, real government. A bill of rights was the least of their worries.

In addition to being busy with other things, a majority of the congressmen were Federalists; they had from the beginning seen no compelling need for a bill of rights. In Philadelphia, delegates to the Federal Convention had dismissed the suggestion for a bill of rights for a variety of reasons. Some pointed out that most states had bills of rights in their own constitutions. Others pointed out that the Constitution included the essential protections. It specifically prohibited bills of attainder (legislative acts by which a citizen loses all civil rights) and ex post facto laws (any law that punishes deeds that were not illegal at the time they were committed), and it required writs of habeas corpus (a protection against arbitrary imprisonment) and trial by a local jury in criminal cases; treason was closely defined.

For his part, Alexander Hamilton worried that a list of

*James Madison (The Bettmann Archive)*

fundamental liberties would inevitably suggest that the government had control in spheres where the Constitution in fact had not given the government any control. Hamilton reasoned that the exceptions to powers not granted might one day provide the grounds for claims to that very power. For example, a provision for freedom of the press might suggest that the government had some right to regulate the press. He also considered a bill of rights absurd in a constitution that was limited to general national concerns, not personal and private concerns. Noah Webster, agreeing with this last point, put it through his satirical mill: Webster urged that a bill of rights ensure "that Congress shall never restrain any inhabitant of America from eating and drinking, at seasonable times, or preventing his lying on his left side, in a long winter's night, or even on his back when he is fatigued by lying on his right."[1]

For his part, James Madison thought Congress must submit a bill of rights to the people—and quickly. If Congress did not act soon, the pressure for another convention might become overwhelming. New York's circular letter to all of the other states, one of the trade-offs for ratification by New York, had formally proposed a second federal convention, a prospect that alarmed Madison. Such a convention, with Antifederalists in control, might easily undo the fragile accord that had been reached in Philadelphia. Or a second convention might draw up a poorly designed bill of rights.

Madison also reasoned that if the Federalists wished to remain in power, they must provide the public with what it wanted. In state after state, the public had said it wanted a bill of rights—North Carolina was *still* withholding its decision on ratification for want of one. Further, a bill of rights would pick up new support for the fledgling government from moderate Antifederalists whose only complaint with the Constitution was the missing bill of rights.

James Madison himself had a campaign pledge to live up to; he had run for Congress against James Monroe, an Antifederalist, who had appealed to the voters by painting Madison as a Federalist wedded to the Constitution as it stood.

Still, James Madison's support for a bill of rights was not wholly political. True, he had not originally seen a need for a bill of rights, but his view had been profoundly reshaped by the ratification battle. Madison had been dismayed when the Massachusetts ratification convention had approved the Constitution with recommended amendments. But he realized that subsequent amendments were far better than previous amendments, and he urged Federalists in other states to follow the Massachusetts model to ensure ratification. With the national government set up, Federalists had a debt of honor to pay.

James Madison's views on a bill of rights were also altered by Thomas Jefferson. Appointed minister to France in 1785, Jefferson had devoted considerable energy to his correspondence with friends at home, which kept him well informed about opinions and events in the states. Responding to a letter from Madison outlining the results of the Federal Convention, Jefferson expressed his pleasure with the Constitution's design as a whole, but of the things he did not like, the absence of a bill of rights was at the top of the list: ". . . a bill of rights is what the people are entitled to against every government on earth, general or particular, and what no government should refuse, or rest on inference."[2] Favoring establishment of the Constitution but convinced that it must contain a bill of rights, Jefferson came up with a ploy by which both might be had: he proposed that nine states ratify the Constitution, thus bringing the new government into being, while four states reject it, thus forcing the new government to provide a bill of rights in order to bring the last states into the union. Madison's original view that a bill of rights was merely a "paper barrier" began to soften. He came to believe that individual rights embedded in the Constitution might one day be seen as the essential grounding for a free society. Properly articulated, those rights might also provide the judicial branch with guidelines for protecting the individual from the onslaughts of control by the majority.

Just as our system of government has its roots in the British experience, so too does our bill of rights. The concept that government may not tamper with certain rights of the individual was first asserted in Magna Carta, the agreement extracted from King John by his barons in 1215. Most of that document's sixty-three chapters concern limitations on specific baronial obligations. But two provisions have endured beyond that time. Chapter 12 holds that "Scutage or aid shall be levied in our kingdom only by the common counsel of our kingdom."[3] (*Scutage* was the feudal term for a payment in lieu of military service.) In essence, the chapter is the precursor to the byword "No taxation without representation" of the American Revolution. Chapter 39 states that "No free man shall be captured or imprisoned or disseised or outlawed or exiled or in any way destroyed . . . except by the lawful judgment of his peers and by the law of the land."[4] It is the precursor to the Due Process Clause of the Fifth Amendment, which guarantees that an individual can be deprived of life, liberty, or property only after being found guilty of a crime in a court of law.

More than four and a half centuries later, Parliament passed the Bill of Rights of 1689. Like Magna Carta, it was drawn up in response to the abuses Englishmen had suffered at the hands of seventeenth-century kings. However, the Bill of Rights of 1689 was unlike Magna Carta in two respects: it was much more concerned with individual liberties, but its provisions were phrased as liberties the government "ought to"—not "shall"—protect.

By then, Americans had developed their own, more so-phisticated concepts of individual rights and documents protecting them. Using their colonial charters, which acknowledged that the colonists could exercise all the rights of Englishmen and provided for colonial assemblies, American legislatures had begun passing statutes that specified basic rights. The Massachusetts Body of Liberties, enacted in 1641, carefully enunciated the people's rights and liberties as a protection against the capriciousness of their own representatives. It became the model for similar enactments throughout the colonies.

The colonies and the mother country would haggle over the rights of Englishmen until the Revolution. Then, mindful of their experience, Americans were even more careful to define the boundaries of government and make explicit the individual's fundamental rights when organizing their state governments.

To draw up a bill of rights, James Madison had before him the more than two hundred amendments formally recommended by the ratification conventions of New Hampshire, Massachusetts, New York, Virginia, and South Carolina; the amendments published by Antifederalists in Pennsylvania and Maryland; and the amendments submitted by North Carolina. When duplication was taken into account, Americans had cited close to a hundred alterations they wanted made. Ultimately, all of the recommendations concerning individual freedoms found a place in the Bill of Rights. Only the Just Compensation Clause of the Fifth Amendment did not appear among the suggestions from the states.

James Madison was no stranger to the task of outlining individual liberties. At the urging of the Second Continental Congress in May 1776, the colonies had wrested control of local government from the Crown's appointed governors and begun setting up governments of their own. Madison had been a member of the committee that prepared Virginia's constitution and declaration of rights. There he had been able to observe George Mason, author of the Virginia Declaration of Rights.

In many respects, Virginia had been the pacesetter. It was the first state to respond to the May 1776 resolution of Congress. It was the first state to formally call for independence. It was the first state to make its bill of rights a part of its constitution. This last is especially important. Constitutions are harder to change than legislative acts; including a bill of rights in a constitution protects the protections themselves.

James Madison presented his draft of a bill of rights for the Constitution to the House of Representatives on June 8. His proposals were grouped in nine sections specifying alterations to the text of the Constitution itself. In addition to individual rights and liberties, he offered a statement on the theory of government to preface the Constitution and proposals regarding congressional size and compensation. The entire matter languished until July 21. Then, prodded by Madison, the House set up a select committee, composed of one representative from each state, to consider the amendments. The committee reported a week later, having retained the substance but tightened the language of Madison's proposals. After being debated by the entire House—again only at Madison's prodding—another committee was formed to put the amendments into finished form. It organized the proposals into seventeen amendments that, if ratified, would be appended to the end of the Constitution rather than woven in, as Madison had originally envisioned. Presented to the House on August 24, the amendments went to the Senate without further change that same day.

As in the House, an attempt was made in the Senate to postpone the whole matter of a bill of rights, but the motion failed. In the course of its debate on the Bill of Rights, the

Senate further refined the language of the proposed amendments, and the seventeen articles reported were reorganized into twelve. Four elements were deleted: the statement of the theory of government; a limit on appeals; a firm reiteration of the separation of powers; and a prohibition against *state* violations of the rights of conscience, freedom of speech, freedom of the press, and trial by jury in criminal cases. This last Madison regarded as "the most valuable amendment in the whole list."[5]

The Senate finished its work on September 9, and a conference committee was set up to reconcile the House and Senate versions of the twelve amendments they had both agreed to submit for ratification. The final form of the proposed bill of rights was approved by the House on September 24, by the Senate the next day, and transmitted to the states by President Washington on October 2, 1789.

Surprisingly, little is known about the debates surrounding ratification of the Bill of Rights in the states. Five states—New Hampshire, New York, New Jersey, Pennsylvania, and Delaware—turned down the first two proposed amendments, which concerned the size of the House of Representatives and compensation for congressmen. Failing to win enough support to be ratified, they did not become a part of the Bill of Rights. The Virginia House of Delegates endorsed the Bill of Rights by a wide margin in December 1789, but the state Senate at first balked. Antifederalists were dismayed by the proposed bill of rights, viewing its protections of both individuals and the states as weak. Two years later, on December 15, 1791, the Virginia Senate finally relented. The tenth state to ratify, Virginia provided the three-fourths majority to put the Bill of Rights into effect. As secretary of state, Thomas Jefferson notified the states in a curiously offhand fashion. On March 1, 1792, he wrote to the governors:

I have the honor to send you herein enclosed, two copies duly authenticated, of an Act concerning certain fisheries of the United States, and for the regulation and government of the fishermen employed therein: also of an Act to establish the post office and post roads within the United States; also the ratifications by three-fourths of the Legislatures of the Several States, of certain articles in addition and amendment of the Constitution of the United States, proposed by Congress to the said Legislatures, and of being with sentiments of the most perfect respect, your Excellency's &.[6]

Connecticut and Georgia did not ratify the Bill of Rights; nor, technically, did Massachusetts. Records from the two houses of the Massachusetts legislature indicate that both the House and the Senate agreed to nine of the amendments—they too rejected the articles concerning congressional size and salaries. What is now the tenth amendment was also rejected. But they did not pass a bill declaring ratification of the other nine or notify Secretary of State Jefferson. Only in 1939 did Massachusetts, Connecticut, and Georgia formally ratify the Bill of Rights.

The First Amendment begins with two prohibitions concerning religion. The Establishment Clause forbids the government from setting up a national religion—we now speak of the separation of church and state. The Free Exercise Clause forbids the government from interfering with the individual's choice of how, or whether, to worship. Some congressmen worried that such an amendment would be the undoing of religion altogether. Still, the principles that government ought not to sponsor religion or in any way direct its observation had been laid down earlier. Many colonists had fled to America because of religious intolerance. Thinking about English history, all knew that religion had sparked strife—even war. The freedoms of speech and of the press were included in reaction to England's libel law. Libel—

speech or writing that misrepresents the facts and damages an individual's or a group's reputation—should not be tolerated, but England's law was so stringent that it gave the government a means to punish anyone whose views displeased those in power. As for the right "to assemble, and to petition the government for a redress of grievances," the events leading up to the Revolution had showed the necessity for this safeguard.

The right to bear arms, or weapons, which is protected in the Second Amendment, was a right first protected in the English Bill of Rights of 1689.

England's practice of housing soldiers in the homes of private citizens prior to the Revolution had been particularly resented by the colonists. That gave rise to the Third Amendment. It forbids the practice when there is no war unless the homeowner's consent has been obtained; during wartime, it can be done only in accordance with a law passed for those circumstances. Both outgrowths of the colonial experience, they still reflect American values in putting the civilian sector above the military.

The British had used writs of assistance and general warrants during the colonial period as a means to find contraband. They required no specification of what was being sought or suspicion that a law had been broken. Their indiscriminate use had often bloomed into appalling abuse. The "List of Infringements and Violation of those Rights," prepared by a Boston Committee of Correspondence in 1772, claimed that "officers . . . break thro' the sacred rights of the *Domicil*, ransack men's houses, destroy their securities, carry off their property, and . . . commit the most horred murders."[7] Thus the Fourth Amendment. The amendment's protection against seizure was first asserted in Magna Carta, but it was Americans who first asserted the protection against search.

The Fifth Amendment concerns the rights of the accused.

It requires indictment by a grand jury, which determines that there is enough evidence to suggest that an individual has broken the law. It also protects the individual from double jeopardy (being tried more than once for the same crime) and self-incrimination (having to testify against oneself). Its Due Process Clause—"No person shall . . . be deprived of life, liberty, or property, without due process of law"—evolved from the phrase "law of the land" in Magna Carta. Over the centuries, "due process of the law" was occasionally used in place of "law of the land," and the phrases were considered synonymous. But with time, distinctions between the terms began to emerge. In 1787, Alexander Hamilton recognized that "due process" extended far greater protection. A person could not be deprived of rights or property by a legislative act alone; he or she must first be given a trial.

The Just Compensation Clause, at the end of the Fifth Amendment, requires payment for property taken for public use. The one provision in the Bill of Rights that was not among those recommended by the states, it had been first cited as a basic right in the Massachusetts Body of Liberties, drawn up in 1641.

The Sixth, Seventh, and Eighth Amendments are also concerned with the rights of the accused. They lay out specific requirements for court proceedings—in both criminal and civil cases. Even in the mid-seventeenth century, the right to counsel—that is, representation by a lawyer—was recognized as essential if the accused were to have a fair trial. Indeed, the right was first protected in the Massachusetts Body of Liberties. And those found guilty were not to be subject to inappropriate or inhumane punishment—"excessive fines" or "cruel and unusual punishment."

The Ninth Amendment was written to address Alexander Hamilton's concern that a bill of rights might endanger those rights not explicitly stated. The amendment makes clear that the first eight amendments list only a few of the many individual rights that the government cannot abridge.

The Tenth Amendment reiterates the framers' intention to create a federal system, with the national government having authority in specific areas, the states having authority in all other areas. While the House of Representatives was debating this issue—called reserved powers—a motion was made to use the term "powers not *expressly* delegated." James Madison replied that "it was impossible to confine a government to the exercise of express powers; there must necessarily be admitted powers by implication, unless the constitution descended to recount every minutia."[8] The motion was again raised in the House, then raised during the Senate debate, but it was voted down in every instance. The framers knew that the nation would grow and change. What they did not know was *how* it would grow and change. The Constitution must allow the national government to respond to new and different needs.

# 6
# LATER AMENDMENTS

Since ratification of the first ten amendments—the Bill of Rights—to the Constitution, another sixteen have been ratified. Some seem essentially technical. But all of the amendments, by virtue of the difficulty of the amending process, grew out of essential needs, dramas, passions, or revisions in the national consensus.

The Eleventh Amendment is a direct response to a 1793 Supreme Court case. When it exercised its jurisdiction in *Chisholm* v. *Georgia*, in which a citizen of South Carolina sued the state of Georgia over an inheritance, all of the states were so angered and worried that Congress reacted quickly. The amendment prohibits federal courts from hearing cases lodged against a state by a citizen of another state. Since passage, the amendment has been construed so as to prohibit suits against states by their own citizens or by a foreign state. However, cities and counties, as well as government corporations of a state, are suable. In addition, state government officials are suable.

Highly technical prose belies the dramatic origin of the Twelfth Amendment. In 1800, presidential candidates Thomas Jefferson and Aaron Burr tied in the electoral college voting. The House of Representatives was so long in deciding who would be president that many feared that no decision would

*Opponents of the Equal Rights Amendment, led by Phyllis Schlafly, demonstrating in front of the White House in 1977 (Associated Press)*

be made by the time of the inauguration, in March. The amendment altered the system devised by the framers in requiring that choices for president and vice president be designated.

More than sixty years would elapse before the amending process was used again. Then, the Thirteenth, Fourteenth, and Fifteenth amendments were passed in rapid succession. Slavery, divisive for the framers, had divided the nation almost seventy-five years later. The first two of these amendments grew out of *Scott* v. *Sandford,* a case ruled on by the Supreme Court in 1857. Dred Scott's attorneys asserted that their client was released from slavery when his master took him to an area where slavery was not permitted in accordance with the Missouri Compromise. But the court ruled that slaves were by definition not citizens, either of the United States or of the individual states; further, the Court held that Congress could not outlaw slavery in the territories.

In 1863, President Abraham Lincoln had declared in the Emancipation Proclamation that slaves in the Confederate States were free. The Thirteenth Amendment extended the abolition of slavery to all states. The Fourteenth Amendment made all former slaves citizens of the United States and thus of the state in which they lived. States are prohibited from depriving any citizen of life, liberty, or property without due process of law. Nor may states enact laws that extend rights to one person but not to another—the Equal Protection Clause. Section 2 of the Fourteenth Amendment serves as a mechanism for penalizing a state that does not give its citizens voting rights in national elections: representation in Congress would be reduced. (This section was never employed.) Section 3 was intended as a way to prevent officers of the federal government who had joined the Confederacy from holding a national post again. However, this provision could be set aside by a two-thirds vote in the House and the

Senate. Section 4 affirmed the validity of the Union's Civil War debt and voided Confederacy war debts. Further, it stipulated that former slaveholders could claim no compensation for the slaves they had lost.

Section 1 of the Fourteenth Amendment has without doubt had the most profound and enduring effect. By it, citizens are protected from the arbitrary actions of their state legislatures. The Due Process Clause was at last binding on state governments, not just on the national government. Further, by a process called incorporation, Section 1 of the Fourteenth Amendment has over the past century served as the stepping stone by which states have been required to respect most of the protections laid out in the federal Bill of Rights. At this time, the only rights that have not been incorporated are the Fifth Amendment's right to a grand jury indictment and the Seventh Amendment's right to a jury trial in civil cases in which more than twenty dollars is at issue. James Madison would have been pleased.

The Constitution had left to the states the right to set qualifications for who might vote. The Fifteenth Amendment does not tamper with that right, but it does stipulate that no requirement can be established on the basis of race. Initially, the Supreme Court voided only those state voting requirements that explicitly referred to race. Beginning in the mid-1890s, seven Southern states got around the Fifteenth Amendment by setting high property, taxpaying, or educational requirements, which denied the vote to most blacks and many whites. So-called grandfather clauses, giving the vote to any descendant of a person entitled to vote on January 1, 1867, reenfranchised the whites who could not meet the voting requirements. Grandfather clauses were ruled unconstitutional by the Supreme Court in 1915.

In 1894, Congress passed a law by which revenues could be raised from a tax on personal income. In 1895, a divided

Supreme Court, in *Pollock* v. *Farmer's Loan and Trust Company*, held that a tax on incomes derived from property was a direct tax; as such, it was in violation of Article I, Sections 2 and 9 of the Constitution. Later Supreme Court decisions began to regard an income tax as an indirect tax, and thus constitutional. But by then the Sixteenth Amendment was in the works. Congress would not be at the mercy of a fickle Court.

Not until 1919, with ratification of the Seventeenth Amendment, were senators elected directly by the people rather than by state legislatures. To some degree, as states loosened their voting requirements, giving more and more people the franchise, or vote, it was perceived that senators should be popularly elected. But the amendment gained additional impetus from the failures of the mode chosen by the framers: state legislatures often deadlocked, with the result that Senate seats were occasionally vacant; further, instances of senators gaining their seats by buying the votes of state legislators were not unheard of.

The Eighteenth Amendment prohibited "the manufacture, sale, or transportation"—and thus the consumption—of alcoholic beverages. Many Americans, known as prohibitionists, had worked hard since the early nineteenth century to outlaw alcoholic beverages on the grounds that they sapped, even destroyed, the consumer. In 1846, Maine adopted prohibition laws, and within the next ten years, another twelve states followed suit. But the movement waned, and by 1900 there were but five so-called dry states.

America's entry into World War I gave the prohibitionists a new argument: they maintained that grain was desperately needed for the war effort, not for the manufacture of liquor. In 1917, Congress passed laws limiting the manufacture of liquor for the duration of the war. In addition, the Eighteenth Amendment was readied and sent to the states for ratification. By January 1919, the necessary three-fourths of the states had agreed.

Like the prohibition movement, the woman suffrage movement needed decades before an amendment giving women the vote could be gained. In 1869, two organizations were formed: the National Woman Suffrage Association, led by Elizabeth Cady Stanton and Susan B. Anthony, a group that urged amending the Constitution; and the American Woman Suffrage Association, led by Lucy Stone and her husband, Henry Blackwell, a more conservative group that worked to get the states to grant women the vote.

The Territory of Wyoming had given women voting rights in 1869 and continued to do so when it became a state. But while other states—mostly in the West—followed Wyoming's example, many did not. Because states were reluctant to extend the vote to women, the two woman suffrage organizations merged in 1890 to form the National American Woman Suffrage Association, and the new group turned its attention to Congress. The movement had the support of Progressives, who saw women's outlook dovetailing with their own. Giving women the vote would help Progressives pass legislation in other areas that concerned them—for example, prohibition. A woman suffrage amendment had been introduced in every Congress since 1878. In 1918, the House of Representatives approved the amendment—one representative was brought on a stretcher to vote. But the Senate did not agree to it until 1919. The Nineteenth Amendment was ratified in 1920. But one political scientist suggests that the timing may have been critical. Had the amendment gone to the states a few years later, when the Progressive movement began to decline, it might have failed.[1]

Often called the "lame duck" amendment, the Twentieth Amendment advanced the dates for newly elected officials to take office from March to January. The alteration bespeaks the dramatic change in the tempo of American life since the writing of the Constitution. Too many important issues arose in the time between early-November elections and March. "Lame ducks," officials who hold office after losing an election, should not be making all those decisions. The Constitution does not specify when newly elected officials are to take office. The date was fixed by a 1788 act of the Confederation Congress. But because the Constitution does specify the length of terms, a change of date would shorten those terms by several months in the year of the transition. Thus an amendment was needed.

The Prohibition Era had begun in 1920, when the Eighteenth Amendment went into effect. Before long, it was clear that prohibition was a force more destructive than constructive. Powerful underworld gangs sprang up to supply the public with liquor, and so extensive was the demand that the gangs grew rich. Vying for control of the lucrative liquor market, they precipitated a period of extreme violence.

Many otherwise law-abiding citizens felt no compunction about defying the law. They viewed prohibition as a violation of their right to set their own standards for personal conduct.

Between the gangs and the public was the government. It simply could not provide enough law-enforcement agents to cope with the sheer number of violations. Some agents chose not to enforce the law because so many Americans firmly believed the law wrong. Other agents accepted bribes for not reporting violations.

The Twenty-first Amendment, by which the Eighteenth was repealed, gained support not just because of the corrosive effects of prohibition on American life. The onset of the Great Depression, in 1929, made repeal even more attractive, for the government would be able to raise much-needed revenues by its tax on alcoholic beverages. The amendment did not mandate that states repeal prohibition;

indeed, Section 2 assured federal help to states that chose to remain dry. But one by one, states repealed their prohibition laws. Mississippi was the last to do so in 1966. Now only a few areas of the country are dry by virtue of local laws.

The Twenty-second Amendment, passed in 1951, specifies that no president may hold office for more than two terms. It also specifies that anyone who serves out more than two years of a presidential term is eligible for election as president only once. The amendment was proposed and ratified with President Franklin Roosevelt in mind. At the time of his death, he was serving his fourth term in office.

By the Twenty-third Amendment, residents of the District of Columbia—the framers' "ten Miles square"—were permitted to vote for the president. Still, they were given no representatives. The District of Columbia is represented by Congress as a whole, as outlined in Article I, Section 8 of the Constitution.

The Twenty-fourth Amendment prohibited poll, or head, taxes. Such taxes, which a voter was required to pay in order to vote, had proved a handy device for states wishing to keep the poor and blacks from participating in elections.

With the Twenty-fifth Amendment, provision was made for filling a vacancy in the office of vice president. (Previously, the office remained vacant until the end of the term.) The amendment also provides for the vice president to serve as acting president when the president is temporarily unable to carry out his duties. The president's nomination for a vice president requires approval by a majority of both houses of Congress. Ratified after the assassination of President John Kennedy, the amendment was used twice in succession in the 1970s. When President Richard Nixon's vice president, Spiro Agnew, was forced to resign from office in 1973, the amendment provided the means for the appointment of Gerald Ford as vice president. The next year, when President Nixon was forced to resign, Ford became president and, by the terms of the amendment, Nelson Rockefeller became vice president.

Before ratification of the Twenty-sixth Amendment, ten states had extended the vote to citizens below the age of twenty-one. Congress had lowered the voting age to eighteen in 1970. The law recognized that eighteen-year-olds, who were regarded as adults in civil and criminal law and who, if male, were at that time subject to the draft, should enjoy the right to elect their representatives. But in 1971, the Supreme Court ruled in *Oregon* v. *Mitchell* that the law could apply only to federal elections. To give eighteen-year-olds the vote in state and local elections as well, the Court held, states must individually enact legislation or the Constitution must be amended.

Amending the Constitution is not an easy process. As devised by the framers, both steps in the process—approval by Congress and then by the states—require extraordinary majorities. The system can thus make a minority the controlling force. But its virtue lies in the fact that the system ensures the legitimacy and acceptance of the Constitution as it evolves to reflect felt needs, and it has for the most part allowed the Constitution to remain an uncluttered summary of broad principles. The process holds Americans together by necessitating the building of consensus. Most recently, we have seen an amendment fail for want of that consensus.

When the suffragists were first struggling to expand the rights of women, many wanted an amendment to the Constitution that would give women equal rights. But many others thought that the times were not ripe for such an amendment. A women's suffrage amendment, they maintained, might not be ratified, but its prospects were much better than those for an equal rights amendment. Armed with the vote, they went on, women could eventually get equal rights by electing representatives sympathetic to such legislation.

Beginning in 1923, an amendment calling for equal rights for women has been raised in every Congress. In 1950 and 1953, the amendment was passed by the Senate, though with a restriction that nullified its effect. Senator Carl T. Hayden managed to attach what was called the Hayden rider, which held that an equal rights amendment "shall not be construed to impair any rights, benefits or exemptions now or hereafter conferred by law, upon persons of female sex."[2]

All the while, the amendment never reached the House floor because Representative Emanuel Cellar kept it bottled up in the House Judiciary Committee. Not until 1970 did the amendment reach the House floor, where it passed. Then the Senate voted it down. Finally, in 1972, the ERA, as it was known, was passed by the necessary two-thirds of each house of Congress.

"Equality of rights under the law shall not be denied or abridged by the United States or by any state on account of sex." On its face, the proposed twenty-seventh amendment hardly seems revolutionary. Indeed, twenty-two states quickly ratified it. But by 1973, opposition to the amendment grew more organized and more vocal, and the pace of ratification slowed. Thirty states had ratified by the end of 1973; three more did so in 1974; one ratified in 1975, none in 1976, and one—by a margin of one vote—in 1977. At thirty-five states, the movement had stalled. Opponents of the ERA managed to get five states to rescind—that is, take back—their ratification. Congress voted to extend the deadline until June 30, 1982, and, further, voted that states could not rescind their ratification. Still, the new deadline came around with not even one of the three more state ratifications needed for the amendment to pass.

What happened? Many opponents maintained that the

amendment was unnecessary. What with the Due Process and Equal Protection clauses of the Fifth and Fourteenth amendments and recent legislation like the Equal Pay Act of 1963 and Title VII of the Civil Rights Act of 1964, women's rights were protected. But, they went on, such an amendment threatened many laws that gave women essential protections—for example, labor laws regulating the hours women could work, how much weight a woman could be asked to lift; family laws regulating everything from maternity benefits to child custody, division of property, and alimony payments in divorce. That women would be subject to military service evoked particularly stiff opposition.

The ERA's proponents held that the amendment was essential. They pointed out that the Fifth and Fourteenth amendments had not prevented courts from upholding laws—an estimated eight hundred federal ones alone[3]—based on gender distinctions. Further, the Equal Pay Act, Title VII, and similar legislation did not affect all women and had not been well understood or well enforced. They maintained that laws should neither deny nor confer rights solely on the basis of gender. For example, laws providing for maternity leaves would remain untouched because only women can bear children; but laws pertaining to the raising of children must apply equally to men and women because gender does not limit that role. Finally, rights go hand in hand with responsibilities. Yes, proponents of the amendment agreed, women would be subject to the draft—and draft exemptions—just as men were.

Seen simply in the political context, the failure of the ERA is chalked up in part to the poor national organization of the amendment's supporters. Others point out that the weak economy of the late 1970s may have given rise to fears that the amendment would set off a great surge of women looking for work in an already tight job market.

But ultimately, the amendment failed because a significant

minority of Americans was not ready for it. The bland text of the amendment unleashed a welter of intense, often uncomprehended and unarticulated, anxieties about American life, about appropriate roles for men and women, even about femininity and masculinity. What would become of our society if women were encouraged or forced out of their role as nurturers of the family? they asked. What would become of traditional American values if women went to war alongside men? Could the United States even win such a war?

Proponents of the ERA acknowledged that not all the effects—legal and social—of the amendment could be anticipated. No doubt, women's perception of their world and their place in it would change as their perception of rights and responsibilities changed. No doubt, too, men's perception of their world and their place in it would change, for it is instinctive to strive for equilibrium.

The ERA has not been reintroduced, but it continues to color Americans' personal and political thinking. Even though the amendment failed, its proposal signifies yet another step in the evolution of our society—consider the ways women can and do participate in American life now as compared with two hundred years ago. At heart, social evolution is what constitutional amendments are all about. On occasion the Constitution has ceased to fit as American ideals about the role and system of government and individual rights are refined. The amending process pays respect to the framers' faith in their posterity and their own ideals alike.

# 7
# THE JUDICIARY

Of all the branches of the national government outlined in the Constitution, the judicial branch was the sketchiest. Delegates to the Federal Convention had been concerned that inferior federal courts scattered throughout the states might be regarded as a physical encroachment on the states and thereby provide a reason for rejecting the Constitution. They therefore ducked the issue by leaving the establishment of inferior courts up to Congress. The delegates specified in Article III, Section 2, the kinds of cases over which the Supreme Court would have original jurisdiction—that is, the power to rule on cases when they first arise. As for appellate jurisdiction—the power to rule on appeals—the Constitution allows Congress to tinker with that list.

The Judiciary Act of 1789 filled in the vague outline. The Supreme Court was to be composed of a chief justice and five associate justices. As for inferior courts, the nation was divided into thirteen districts and three circuits, each with lower federal courts. Circuit courts, sitting twice a year, were presided over by two Supreme Court justices and a district court judge. Three judicial levels—district courts, circuit courts, and the Supreme Court—and two types of judges—district judges and Supreme Court justices—afforded a system acceptable to both Federalists and Antifederalists.

*John Marshall, Chief Justice of the United States Supreme Court
[1801–35] (Library of Congress)*

Supreme Court justices, in riding circuit, would be forced to see legal problems in the locales in which they arose—a principle important to Antifederalists. District judges and Supreme Court justices, by working together in the circuit courts, would give uniformity to legal interpretation and thus cohesion to the nation—an essential goal in Federalist eyes.

There was some grumbling about the Judiciary Act of 1789. To enforce the Constitution's Supremacy Clause, Section 25 gave federal courts the power to overturn state court rulings. Those who feared that the national government would swallow up the states saw Section 25 as the tool for that. Nonetheless, Congress passed the act. And as the nation has grown, both in terms of land mass and population, other judiciary acts have been passed to fit the judicial branch to new needs. Nowadays, some six hundred judges staff district courts. Each of eleven circuit courts throughout the nation is staffed by four to fourteen appeals court judges. There is still only one Supreme Court, now composed of nine justices. But all of the Supreme Court's justices take part in the Court's rulings; the workload is not divided.

The Supreme Court can be seen as the tip of the judicial iceberg. Many cases never come before the Supreme Court. Of about five thousand petitions submitted for its consideration each year, the Court agrees to hear fewer than two hundred cases. In addition to original and appellate jurisdiction as defined by the Constitution and Congress's various judiciary acts, the Supreme Court hears cases that challenge the constitutionality of various laws.

Although the Court rules on such a small percentage of all the cases heard in the United States, it has commanded a seemingly disproportionate share of the public's attention. Poised to keep the entire governmental structure in balance, ensuring that the executive and legislative branches do not exceed the bounds set for them by the Constitution, the

Court hears cases that touch on—and sometimes sum up—philosophical and political questions of the times. And while a ruling pertains to the case before the Court, that ruling will echo through American life because of *stare decisis*. The formal legal term for precedent, *stare decisis* refers to the practice of building on and extending the reasoning for previous judgments in current cases. Thus a judge in a lower court, when presented with a case similar to one decided by the Supreme Court, will make a ruling in conformance to the Supreme Court decision. By following precedent, a judicial system provides for the development of a logical, consistent body of law. Indeed, so strong is this inclination that only in the mid-1850s did the Supreme Court begin overturning precedents.

At first, the Supreme Court did not play an especially large role in American political life. It heard but sixty cases in its first twelve years of operation. John Jay, the first chief justice, gave up his post in 1795. He found the circuit-riding onerous (only in 1869 were Supreme Court justices freed of that duty); further, the job seemed a little dull. Oliver Ellsworth, a delegate to the Federal Convention in Philadelphia and sponsor of the Judiciary Act of 1789, held the position for the next four and a half years.

The Court's low profile changed with the third chief justice, John Marshall. In part because the federal judiciary was young, and thus malleable, in part because Marshall served as chief justice from 1801 until his death in 1835, he profoundly affected both the Court's procedures and its position in the federal government. But much of Marshall's enduring legacy to the Court and the country must be attributed to his powerful intellect and ardent nationalism.

Among the most significant cases in American legal history is *Marbury* v. *Madison*. Just before leaving the presidency, John Adams appointed William Marbury a justice of the peace for the District of Columbia, but the appointment papers were not delivered before Thomas Jefferson was inaugurated president. The Jefferson administration would not finalize a Federalist appointment. Marbury sued James Madison, Jefferson's secretary of state, in an effort to gain the documents so that he could take up his position. As author of the Court's decision, handed down in 1803, Marshall allowed that Marbury should be given his papers but that the Supreme Court could not force the Jefferson administration to do so. Marshall's opinion turned on the question of jurisdiction. Section 13 of the Judiciary Act of 1789 gave the Supreme Court original jurisdiction in this type of case—in violation, Marshall asserted, of original jurisdiction as spelled out in the Constitution. In voiding Section 13 of the Judiciary Act of 1789, Marshall asserted what is called judicial review—the power of the Supreme Court to void congressional and executive acts it considers in violation of the Constitution:

> The powers of the legislature are defined and limited; and that those limits may not be mistaken, or forgotten, the constitution is written. To what purpose are powers limited, and to what purpose is that limitation committed to writing, if these limits may, at any time, be passed by those intended to be restrained? The distinction between a government with limited and unlimited powers, is abolished, if those limits do not confine the persons on whom they are imposed, and if acts prohibited and acts allowed, are of equal obligation. It is a proposition too plain to be contested, that the constitution controls any legislative act repugnant to it; or, that the legislature may alter the constitution by an ordinary act.
>
> Between these alternatives there is no middle ground. The constitution is either a superior paramount law, unchangeable by ordinary means, or it is on a level with ordinary legislative acts, and like other acts, is alterable when the legislature shall please to alter it. . . .

It is emphatically the province and duty of the judicial branch to say what the law is.[1]

Eighteen years later, the Marshall court established judicial review of state legislation in *Cohens* v. *Virginia*. The Cohen brothers had sold lottery tickets in Virginia, a violation of Virginia law. The Cohens defended their activities on the basis of a congressional act permitting the sale of lottery tickets in the District of Columbia. The Court ruled in Virginia's favor. Nonetheless, many irate observers maintained that the Supreme Court had no right to hear the case in the first place, that it was meddling in a state's own affairs.

Judicial review infuriated many people. If legislators and presidents were on occasion subject to errors of judgment and wisdom, so too were justices. If the judiciary could void legislative and executive acts, then the legislature and executive ought to be able to void judicial decisions.

Thomas Jefferson was among those profoundly unsympathetic to judicial review. To his mind, the entire idea was wrongheaded. He believed that the Constitution clearly defined the boundaries of the executive and legislative branches and that presidents and congressmen were as competent as justices to recognize those boundaries. Jefferson also had an abiding faith in the people. He believed that they could be trusted to respect minority rights, to assess correctly the propriety of the actions of their representatives, and to demand alterations when needed. Jefferson saw the Court as a dangerous foil to all that democracy is about; it stripped the citizenry of its right to make decisions and, in doing so, closed off the public debate by which a nation sets its course. There were checks on the executive and legislative branches—ultimately, the people could expel their president and representatives from office. But where were the checks on the judicial branch, staffed as it is with unelected and virtually unremovable justices? "I do not charge the Judges with wilful and ill-intentioned error," Jefferson wrote, "but honest error must be arrested, where its toleration leads to public ruin. As for the safety of society we must commit honest maniacs to Bedlam, so judges should be withdrawn from the bench, whose erroneous biases are leading us to dissolution."[2]

Thomas Jefferson would not be the last to rail at judicial review. In 1912, Theodore Roosevelt complained bitterly that "by the abuse of power to declare laws unconstitutional the courts have become a law-making instead of law-enforcing agency."[3] Roosevelt proposed the recall of judicial decisions. The idea resurfaced two decades later, in the form of a Senate proposal to permit the overturning of a Court decision by a two-thirds vote in Congress taken after one intervening election—thus giving the public the chance to elect someone who would support their views on the judicial decision in question. A different means by which to appeal Supreme Court decisions was advanced in 1963 by the Council of State Governments. It urged the adoption of an amendment by which a Court of the Union would convene at the request of any five nonadjacent states. Composed of the chief justices of each state's highest court, the Court of the Union would rule on whether a particular Supreme Court decision had been properly a matter for the Supreme Court. Judgments of the Court of the Union would be binding on the Supreme Court. The Council's proposed amendment died upon presentation to the American Bar Association.

Rankled by the concept of judicial review but perceiving it to be unassailable, many have looked for other ways to clip the wings of the Court. Over the years, efforts have been made to confine the Court through procedure—that is, the way the Court functions within itself. Bills to change the Court's appellate jurisdiction come before Congress with numbing regularity—nowadays, a host of such bills concern the Court's jurisdiction in cases concerning laws on abortion. Many proposals have also been made to require an extraordinary majority or even unanimity among the justices for Court rulings in specific kinds of cases. Other bills would alter the makeup of the Court. A requirement of previous judicial experience, mandatory retirement age, election of justices for defined terms—all have had an enduring appeal for some Court critics.

No doubt the most famous plan to alter the Court was that proposed by Franklin Roosevelt. First elected president in 1932, three years after the stock market crashed and set off the Great Depression, Roosevelt believed that the national government must be the catalyst for recovery. But a series of Court decisions handed down in 1935 and 1936 invalidated many of the legislative acts on which his program rested— the National Industrial Recovery Act, the Agricultural Adjustment Act, and the Coal Conservation Act. Congress, like the president, was perturbed, and grumbled about "the nine old men." Often thwarted by a bare majority of the Court, Roosevelt sought to make that majority the minority. In early 1937, he sent to Congress a bill that, on the surface, was intended as a solution to long delays caused by a federal judiciary overloaded with cases. The bill contained a measure that would allow a president to add another justice to a federal court when a justice with ten years of service on that court reached the age of seventy. If passed, that measure would have allowed Roosevelt to make fifty appointments to the lower courts and six to the Supreme Court.

The Senate Judiciary Committee recognized the bill for exactly what it was: Roosevelt's attempt to "pack the court" with liberal justices who would support his program. The committee chided the president and let the bill languish.

In fact, the judicial branch is checked, albeit in subtle ways. Justices are nominated by presidents, but their appointments depend on the Senate's consent. The appointment process thus provides for the selection of justices who reflect the mainstream at any given moment. Although the president nominates justices, the Senate has not been a rubber stamp. Indeed, in the decade 1974–1984, some 20 percent of all judicial nominations were rejected outright or withdrawn because they would be rejected. Once on the bench, judges can be removed by Congress. Impeachment of members of the federal judiciary is rare, but it happens. In 1986, District Judge Harry E. Claiborne was removed from office for filing false tax returns. Four articles of impeachment were voted by the House of Representatives. The Senate convicted him on three of the articles; conviction on even one would have been enough to remove him from the bench.

History has also shown that Court decisions are not necessarily the last word. When a law that the people and their representatives want is overturned, a way can ultimately be found to have that law. In some instances, legislation is simply rewritten. For example, the Court has voided some state laws on the death penalty because of flaws in the procedures by which those sentences were determined. As a consequence, many state legislatures have passed new laws designed to correct procedure.

In other instances, the Court catches up with public opinion. Early in the twentieth century, many laws were passed to protect children and workers by regulating labor practices. Many decisions overturning those laws were handed down before the Court came to agree that the government was properly addressing a legitimate need.

In the end, if a legislative means cannot be found to enact a law, the machinery for amending the Constitution, as provided for in Article V, can be set in motion. The Court is bound by the Constitution. Prohibition came, and went, through the amending process. If Americans should decide that they want their children to have an opportunity to pray in school and they ratify a constitutional amendment to that effect, then schools will set aside time for prayers.

Much of the criticism of the Court stems from the fact that it seems a sort of oligarchy—a small, tightly knit, firmly entrenched group that holds control. Its judgments are often seen as oracular—though Court justices would be the last to claim a superior wisdom. As an example, Justice Louis Brandeis, concerning one of his decisions, observed to his colleague, Felix Frankfurter: "I have never been quite happy about my concurrence. . . . I had not then thought the issues of freedom of speech out. I thought at the subject, not through it."[4]

But much of the criticism comes because of the Constitution's silence on the judiciary. The Court's composition and appellate jurisdiction are not specified. Judicial review is not a power explicitly granted by the Constitution. The Court's defenders maintain that judicial review is an implied power. On the one hand, it is implied by the Supremacy Clause; on the other hand, it is implied by the very limits on the powers of the national government—someone must keep watch to ensure that those bounds are not exceeded. The Court has a role to play because the legislative and executive branches, both beholden to the popular will for their positions, will undoubtedly be subject to powerful pressure from the public. The 1962 Court decision in *Engel* v. *Vitale* held that school prayer, even if not mandatory for students, is unconstitutional. The five parents who brought the case, and their children, were abused by their neighbors. One wonders what legislators would have felt if they had been ultimately responsible for whether prayer would be part of the school day.

The Court's defenders answer those who would change

the Court's face or procedures by pointing out that there is little connection between previous judicial eminence and judicial experience—John Marshall, Louis Brandeis, Felix Frankfurter, and Earl Warren had had none. Many justices have made significant contributions while in their seventies and eighties—take, for example, Oliver Wendell Holmes, who retired as an associate justice at age ninety. The Court's defenders also point out that electing justices for defined terms strips the judicial branch of the independence it must have to do its work. The Court will of necessity often take a course counter to public opinion—it is the Court's job to ensure that majority rule not exceed its bounds. The virtue of the judicial appointment system conceived by the framers is that it provides for a check on emotional surges in public opinion. Changes in the Court's voting systems, requiring extraordinary majorities or unanimity for certain decisions, would put the Court's minority in control. Changes in jurisdiction prevent the Court from protecting rights it is the Court's job to protect, and individual liberties could come to mean different things in different states. For example, restricting the Court's power to hear cases pertaining to apportionment would mean that the vote of a citizen in one state might mean less than the vote of a citizen in another state.

Court rulings have always provoked considerable public debate because they attempt to reconcile the technical aspects of specific laws with the broad principles of the Constitution. "Strict constructionists" believe that the Court should base its decisions on what the laws actually say, not on what they ought to say, and leave the business of writing new laws for new needs to Congress. "Loose constructionists" view that emphasis on the *words* as a violation of the *spirit* of the law. As a case in point, they cite Justice Hugo Black's contention that wiretaps are not mentioned in, and therefore not restricted by, the Fourth Amendment—but of course, wiretaps were unheard of in 1789, when the amendment was written. Another difficulty with strict constructionism is that the Constitution's words mean different things to different people. What one person might consider necessary and proper, another might consider frivolous and invasive. There is, moreover, a gamut of constitutional positions that one can take between the extremes of strict and loose constructionism.

Presidents have always made judicial nominations with a view to selecting justices who are in tune with their own views of where the nation should be going. The Reagan administration has been especially aware of the importance of its judicial appointments. Indeed, some accuse it of using a so-called litmus test—avowal by a prospective appointee of a particular position on specific social issues that may come to the federal courts—in choosing its nominees. In the meantime, the passionate debates about what the Constitution permits, signifying the rich diversity of philosophies the Constitution accommodates, continue.

# 8

# THE IDEAL AND
# THE REALITY

Hewn from the intense debate in Philadelphia during the summer of 1787, the Constitution even then commanded admiration. Thomas Jefferson was one who might have been predisposed against the Constitution: "I own I am not a friend to a very energetic government. It is always oppressive,"[1] he had observed. Still, upon its ratification, he wrote to James Madison, "I sincerely rejoice at the acceptance of our new Constitution by nine states. It is a good canvas, on which some strokes only want retouching."[2]

The Constitution continues to command admiration, for the framers' elegant theoretical invention has worked in nearly two hundred years of practice. Although many of its provisions were drawn from British models, the proposed national government was a peculiarly American invention. Strict enough to remain the bedrock of American political life, the Constitution has proved sufficiently supple to accommodate the extraordinary changes our nation has undergone.

Admiring the Constitution as we do, it is tempting to romanticize it. In the romantic view, the Constitution endures because of an inherent, powerful mystique. But history has shown that even the Constitution's most emphatic assertions have on occasion been flagrantly disregarded. In some instances, the Constitution's sketchiness has given rise to conflict. In yet other instances, the Constitution offers no solutions to the dilemmas that our society confronts. The

*Americans of Japanese ancestry and Japanese residing in the United States arriving at a detention center in Manzanar, California, in 1942 (Associated Press)*

Constitution endures only so long as Americans will not permit its abuse, wisely interpret its general provisions when considering political initiatives, and remember its spirit when choosing among competing social claims. In short, the Constitution draws its vitality from Americans themselves.

The Constitution can easily be abused. Consider the Sedition Act passed in 1798. By it, anyone who criticized government officials or their policies was subject to fines and imprisonment. A clear violation of the right to free speech guaranteed by the First Amendment, the act was firmly supported in federal courts. As one example, Representative Matthew Lyon of Vermont was fined $1,000 and imprisoned for four months for a newspaper letter in which he criticized "the unbounded thirst for ridiculous pomp, foolish adulation, and selfish avarice"[3] of President John Adams.

The concept of judicial review had not at that time been asserted, and the Federalists, both authors and beneficiaries of the law, were in control of the legislative and executive branches. Thus cries that the Sedition Act was unconstitutional drew no immediate response. The American public ultimately put an end to the act. In the 1800 election, they voted the Federalists out of office. President Thomas Jefferson formally pardoned those found guilty of violating the Sedition Act. A Republican Congress did not renew the act and later saw to it that fines were returned.

Abuse of the Constitution is most apt to occur at times of severe stress. Take, for example, the Civil War. The long, bloody battle between Americans served as the background for many congressional and executive acts that, in constitutional terms, were at best tenuous. In 1863, the Court handed down decisions in what are called the Prize Cases, which concerned President Abraham Lincoln's order to seize ships before war had been formally declared. The action was upheld by the slimmest majority of the justices. Soon after, Congress authorized the creation of a tenth seat on the Supreme Court. (Congress would in 1866 reduce the Court to seven seats, then in 1869 expand it to nine seats, the size at which it has since remained.) The tenth seat was justified on the grounds that another circuit was needed to handle the plethora of cases arising from the growth in California. But it also gave Lincoln another Court appointment, thus ensuring a solid majority of justices who would support the measures deemed necessary to win the war.

Late in 1864, L. P. Milligan, a civilian, was arrested in Indiana and found guilty of conspiracy in a court-martial— a military trial. President Andrew Johnson commuted his death sentence to life imprisonment. But Milligan still challenged the action. Ruling on the case in 1866, the Court— including every one of Lincoln's appointees—agreed that the Constitution had been violated. Because the federal courts had still been operating in Indiana, Milligan should not have been brought before a court-martial. Justice David Davis's opinion drew attention to the circumstances when martial law may be employed:

> Martial rule can never exist where the courts are open, and in the proper and unobstructed exercise of their jurisdiction. It is also confined to the locality of actual war. Because, during the late rebellion it could have been enforced in Virginia, where the national authority was overturned and the courts driven out, it does not follow that it should obtain in Indiana, where that authority was never disputed, and justice was always administered. And so in the case of foreign invasion, martial rule may become a necessity in one state, when, in another, it would be "mere lawless violence."[4]

War, in this case World War II, provided the context for another clearly unconstitutional abuse. Several months after the Japanese attack on Pearl Harbor, President Franklin Roosevelt ordered the roundup and internment of 110,000 Americans of Japanese ancestry living on the West Coast.

Over 70 percent were American citizens, yet all were denied their constitutional right to due process—a trial. (Hawaii's 150,000 Japanese Americans were not interned because industry there could not operate without those workers.)[5] The government had no proof of disloyalty, yet in four cases challenging the confiscation of property and internment, the Court reaffirmed Roosevelt's order. But the government's defense rested on false evidence. Further, the American Civil Liberties Union, which was representing the Japanese-American plaintiffs, chose not to build the best case because of its support for the president.

Defined constitutional rights and a judicial system committed to protecting those rights provide Americans with the tools by which to defend themselves. Still, legal proceedings are expensive, and they can seem endless, especially when decisions are appealed. There is also considerable emotional expense. Fred Korematsu, whose conviction for not appearing at a detention center had been upheld by the Supreme Court in 1944, was vindicated only in 1983. For many people, the injustice itself and then the long wait before that injustice was acknowledged would provoke profound bitterness. That Korematsu could say, "I was sent to jail as a criminal, even though I knew I wasn't. I love this country and I belong here," is a testimony to the man, not to the United States.[6]

Even the Constitution's firmest prohibitions demand interpretation, as Chief Justice Roger Taney made clear in his opinion in *Ex parte Merryman*, a case challenging President Lincoln's suspension of the writ of habeas corpus:

The great importance which the framers of the Constitution attached to the privilege of the writ of *habeas corpus* to protect the liberty of the citizen, is proved by the fact that its suspension, except in cases of invasion and rebellion, is first in the list of prohibited power; and even in these cases the power is denied and its exercise prohibited unless the public safety shall require it. It is true that in the cases mentioned Congress is of necessity to judge whether the public safety does or does not require it; and its judgment is conclusive. But the introduction of these words is a standing admonition to the legislative body of the danger of suspending it and of the extreme caution they should exercise before they give the Government of the United States such power over the liberty of a citizen.[7]

The same holds true for the First Amendment's protection of freedom of speech and of the press. It is an established point of law that the amendment does not give an individual in a crowded theater the right to cry "Fire!" when none exists. Nor does the amendment exempt the individual from charges of libel. Today, Americans are grappling with the First Amendment and pornography. Many consider pornography not just distasteful but destructive; they believe it is a direct cause of violence, particularly violence against women. Others worry about efforts to ban it by law. They hold no brief for pornography, but they point out the difficulty in drawing the line between what is and what is not pornographic. They caution that such a step can be the first to government control of all public expression.

The questions raised by even the clearest, firmest passages of the Constitution are many. But questions multiply when the Constitution's vaguer passages are at issue. General principles are subject to a broad range of interpretations and thus provide fertile ground for conflict. The concept of implied powers is one such case that arose early on. When Alexander Hamilton, the first secretary of the treasury, proposed the chartering of the Bank of the United States, he justified its constitutionality on the Necessary and Proper Clause at the end of Article I, Section 8: "To make all Laws which shall be necessary and proper for carrying into Execution the foregoing Powers, and all other Powers vested by this Constitution in the Government of the United States, or in any Department or Officer thereof." Implied powers, with the Bank of the United States as its first point of contention, would highlight the tension between the Federalists, who favored a strong national government, and the Republicans, who favored strong state governments. In 1819, John Marshall defended the concept of implied powers in the decision in *McCulloch* v. *Maryland*, a case challenging state taxes on the Bank of the United States:

> This provision is made in a constitution intended to endure for ages to come, and, consequently, to be adapted to the various crises of human affairs. To have prescribed the means by which government should, in all future time, execute its powers, would have been to change, entirely, the character of the instrument, and give it the properties of a legal code. It would have been an unwise attempt to provide, by immutable rules, for exigencies which, if foreseen at all, must have been seen dimly, and which can be best provided for as they occur.[8]

Today, the national government has an enormous range of concerns never imagined by the framers. The Nuclear Regulatory Commission, the Food and Drug Administration, the Federal Aviation Administration, the Environmental Protection Agency—these are but a few of the government entities that touch every aspect of our lives. As long as the Constitution has force, as long as Americans are convinced that government must be limited and the states should continue to exist, implied powers will be hotly debated.

Writing the Constitution, the framers made the president commander in chief of all of the United States' military forces. They gave to Congress the power to declare war. But the framers' division of war powers has not proved as specific and tidy as it seems on paper. Indeed, American troops have been used overseas more than two hundred times; of those, only five were in wars formally declared by Congress.[9]

For Americans, probably the most provocative of all these undeclared wars was the Vietnam War. American military personnel first went to South Vietnam in 1962. The last left in 1973. At the height of the war, over 500,000 Americans were serving in South Vietnam.

The Vietnam War caused sorrows that are even today keenly felt. Over 59,000 Americans lost their lives or were reported missing in action. Many of those who returned home suffered severe physical and emotional disabilities. The cost of the war, estimated at $160 billion,[10] set in motion the accumulation of a now-staggering national debt that threatens our current and future well-being. Smarting from defeat, Americans continue their oftentimes irrational wrangling and recriminations about what went wrong.

One thing that went wrong was that war was never declared. A declaration of war would have focused the debate about the wisdom of the war itself and clarified the question of Americans' commitment to support such a war. Although American forces were deployed in Vietnam by orders of three presidents—John Kennedy, Lyndon Johnson, and Richard Nixon—Congress was not an unwilling partner. In 1965, by passing the Gulf of Tonkin Resolution, it gave to the president prior approval for any military response he might deem necessary. And for another eight years, Congress approved appropriations to fund the war.

There have been instances when war powers have been held tightly in the presidential grasp. In 1986, President Ronald Reagan sent American bombers to Tripoli, the capital of Libya. The attack was in retaliation for Libya's active support of terrorists. Most Americans supported the president's decision to bomb Tripoli. Still, some were disturbed that he did not consult key congressmen until hours before the attack, when it was too late for congressmen to express any reservations or objections they might have.

The framers understood that in times of war, the nation cannot survive if its forces are under the command of the legislative branch. As technology increases the speed and magnitude of destruction, our safety depends in part on the ability of the president to respond quickly. But by giving Congress the power to declare war and appropriate funds for its prosecution, they intended that Congress serve as a check against a president flexing his military muscle unwisely. With the Vietnam War still fresh in the national mind, Congress passed the War Powers Act in 1973 and has begun asking more questions about American military activities. Still, there is no sense that the manner in which the executive and legislative branches will exercise war powers has been completely sorted out, a fact that is especially disturbing today.

Since the framing of the Constitution, the executive branch has steadily grown in power—a threat, many observers have warned, to the essential equilibrium between it and the legislative branch. Those warnings seemed justified in November 1986, when a scheme formulated by members of the executive branch was uncovered. By it, military equipment was secretly sold to Iran to oil the release of American hostages held in Lebanon by pro-Iranian extremists. Later that same month, another facet of the scheme came to light: profits from the arms sales were sent to Nicaraguan rebels. Even at the beginning of 1987, after two months of allegations, contradictions, accusations, and denials, it was not clear just what had happened, though the spirit if not the letter of applicable laws had been violated—the Arms Export Control Act, the Omnibus Diplomatic Security and Anti-Terrorism Act, and the Boland Amendments prohibited such deals but have provisions that may allow the Reagan administration to claim technical legality for its actions. While Americans try to order the elements of the crisis, we grapple anew with the old constitutional problem: how to limit, balance, and check power and still exercise power.

Debate, frequently fierce over issues where the Constitution is specific or vague, tends to be fiercest over issues where the Constitution is silent. Every generation has its burning questions. One of ours is abortion.

In 1971, arguments challenging the constitutionality of a Texas law prohibiting abortion were heard by the Supreme Court. The plaintiff was Jane Roe, a pseudonym for Norma McCorvey, who had not been able to terminate a pregnancy that resulted from rape. Her attorney argued that pregnancy "is a matter which is of such fundamental and basic concern to the woman involved that she should be allowed to make the choice as to whether to continue or terminate her pregnancy."[11] The defense argued that life begins at conception and that, in addition to the rights of the unborn, the rights of fathers must be considered.

Not until 1973 was a decision rendered. Then, the Court ruled that the Texas abortion law was too broad and violated the right of privacy: "The Constitution does not explicitly mention any right of privacy. In a line of decisions, however . . . the Court has recognized that a right of personal privacy, or a guarantee of certain areas or zones of privacy, does exist under the Constitution."[12] But the decision did not give women a blanket right to abortion. It held that in the first trimester, or three months, of a pregnancy, the woman and her doctor could make the decision to abort the pregnancy. Abortions performed in the second trimester could be subject to state regulations aimed at protecting maternal health alone. But during the last trimester, states could prohibit abortions (except those required to protect the life or health of the mother) because the unborn child is by then sufficiently developed to be able to survive outside the womb.

*Roe* v. *Wade* did not put an end to the intense debate surrounding abortion. Further, the decision did not conclude the Court's consideration of abortion. The same kind of case is sure to arise again because the decision addressed the competing claims of the mother and of the unborn. As technological advances enable physicians to sustain a fetus outside the mother's womb for longer and longer periods, the trimester formula will break down.

Perhaps the United States' greatest national tragedy stems from slavery. That the need to form a nation was stronger in 1787 than the need to end slavery does not detract from the enormous personal loss for countless now-forgotten blacks. The Civil War settled the question, but violently, and only on paper. The Thirteenth, Fourteenth, and Fifteenth amendments corrected the Constitution to agree with the new American consensus that slavery was wrong. Yet it was not until the mid-twentieth century that blacks began to gain the civil rights that, according to the Constitution, had been theirs for a hundred years.

The Court was slow to utilize the tools at hand to protect the rights of blacks. For example, in 1896, the Court held in *Plessy* v. *Ferguson* that states could require the railroads to provide segregated cars. Only Justice John Harlan dissented, sensing that the separate-but-equal provision would "stimulate aggressions more or less brutal and irritating"[13] against the rights of blacks. Reflecting the popular outlook at that time, the Court read law in its narrowest sense.

Not until 1954 did the Court really take the lead, and then it did so in a stunning decision. *Brown* v. *Board of Education* held that separate is inherently unequal. The landmark decision sanctioned what the Civil War had set in motion, and in the process it asked Americans to be finer than they were inclined to be.

More than thirty years after that historic decision, many school systems are not yet fully integrated. But the Court's

1954 ruling proved a watershed in race relations. In the early 1960s, large numbers of private citizens began making personal commitments to social change by giving their own time and energy to bring blacks—and other minorities—into the mainstream of American life. Led by President Johnson, Congress passed the sweeping Civil Rights acts that, twenty years later, Americans are still absorbing. Affirmative action, an effort whereby minorities are given preferential treatment in education and jobs, was instituted. The Constitution is silent about such vigorous efforts to rectify the consequences of so many years of social injustice. Indeed, the constitutionality of affirmative action was challenged in 1977. In *Bakke* v. *University of California*, Allan Bakke asserted that his Fourteenth Amendment right to equal protection of the laws had been violated when the university turned down his application to medical school while less-qualified candidates were accepted to fill affirmative-action quotas for minorities. The Court ruled that while preference may be given to minorities, fixed quotas may not be used.

Minorities still suffer the effects of the racism so long an institution in American life. But that members of both the public and private sector have shown an eagerness to make this centuries-old tragedy truly past history is encouraging, signifying the essential moral grounding of the Constitution on which our nation is based. In the end, that is why we care for the Constitution. Underneath its descriptions of how our government should work lies a philosophy that continues to resonate with the American psyche. Federalism, a limited government of checked and balanced powers, fair laws enforced fairly, personal liberties—all are elements of a government intended to be in the service of the individual, providing at once the orderly society and the freedom we need for our best selves to flourish.

# AFTERWORD

If the framers could see us now, what, one wonders, would they think? Men who looked to the future, they would not be surprised by the extent of progress over two hundred years, though the nature of that progress would amaze them. They would be taken aback by the extent of the United States, including, as it does, Alaska and Hawaii. Confident of the energy a sound government could release in the United States, they would have assumed that the nation would be a superpower.

Looking at the Constitution they wrote for themselves and for us, they would be pleased to see that the structure they devised continues, with few changes, to serve. They might worry that the legislative process is slow and cumbersome for the fast-paced world of today. They would be astonished by all the government agencies and activities unleashed by the Necessary and Proper Clause. They would be appalled by the national debt. They would be deeply distressed that slavery brought Americans into battle against one another.

The astonishing expansion of the powers of the executive branch would precipitate a long and heated debate, and some might make a mental note to themselves that the next time they write a constitution they must be firmer about war powers.

Judicial review would delight some, irritate others, but none of the framers would need to have it explained.

The Antifederalists among them would ruefully note that the

Bill of Rights they had insisted on had, through incorporation, given rise to many restrictions on the states. But they all would have been glad that provisions had been made for amendments. Ultimately, that article has allowed Americans to be true to the Constitution, and the Constitution true to Americans.

# DELEGATES TO THE FEDERAL CONVENTION

*New Hampshire*

Nicholas Gilman
John Langdon

*Massachusetts*

Elbridge Gerry
Nathaniel Gorham
Rufus King
Caleb Strong

*Rhode Island*—none

*Connecticut*

Oliver Ellsworth
William Samuel Johnson
Roger Sherman

*New York*

Alexander Hamilton
John Lansing
Robert Yates

*New Jersey*

David Brearley
Jonathan Dayton
William Churchill Houston
William Livingston
William Paterson

*Pennsylvania*

George Clymer
Thomas Fitzsimons
Benjamin Franklin
Jared Ingersoll
Thomas Mifflin
Gouverneur Morris
Robert Morris
James Wilson

*Delaware*

Richard Bassett
Gunning Bedford
Jacob Broom

John Dickinson
George Read

### Maryland

Daniel Carroll
Daniel of St. Thomas
  Jenifer
Luther Martin
James McHenry
John Francis Mercer

### Virginia

John Blair
James Madison
George Mason
James McClurg
Edmund Randolph
George Washington
George Wythe

### North Carolina

William Blount
William Richardson Davie
Alexander Martin
Richard Dobbs Spaight
Hugh Williamson

### South Carolina

Pierce Butler
Charles Pinckney
Charles Cotesworth
  Pinckney
John Rutledge

### Georgia

Abraham Baldwin
William Few
William Houstoun
William Pierce

# THE CONSTITUTION OF THE UNITED STATES OF AMERICA*

*We the People* of the United States, in Order to form a more perfect Union, establish Justice, insure domestic Tranquility, provide for the common defence, promote the general Welfare, and secure the Blessings of Liberty to ourselves and our Posterity, do ordain and establish this Constitution for the United States of America.

ARTICLE I.

SECTION 1. All legislative Powers herein granted shall be vested in a Congress of the United States, which shall consist of a Senate and House of Representatives.

SECTION 2. The House of Representatives shall be composed of Members chosen every second year by the People of the several States, and the Electors in each State shall have the Qualifications requisite for Electors of the most numerous Branch of the State Legislature.

No Person shall be a Representative who shall not have attained to the Age of twenty-five Years, and been seven Years a Citizen

---

*The text of the Constitution of the United States of America is reprinted from the official version published by the U.S. Government Printing Office (New York: 1976).

of the United States, and who shall not, when elected, be an Inhabitant of that State in which he shall be chosen.

Representatives and direct Taxes shall be apportioned among the several States which may be included within this Union, according to their respective Numbers, which shall be determined by adding to the whole Number of free Persons, including those bound to Service for a Term of Years, and excluding Indians not taxed, three fifths of all other Persons. The actual Enumeration shall be made within three Years after the first Meeting of the Congress of the United States, and within every subsequent Term of ten Years, in such Manner as they shall by Law direct. The Number of Representatives shall not exceed one for every thirty Thousand, but each State shall have at Least one Representative; and until such enumeration shall be made, the State of New Hampshire shall be entitled to chuse three, Massachusetts eight, Rhode-Island and Providence Plantations one, Connecticut five, New-York six, New Jersey four, Pennsylvania eight, Delaware one, Maryland six, Virginia ten, North Carolina five, South Carolina five, and Georgia three.

When vacancies happen in the Representation from any State, the Executive Authority thereof shall issue Writs of Election to fill such Vacancies.

The House of Representatives shall chuse their Speaker and other Officers; and shall have the sole Power of Impeachment.

SECTION 3. The Senate of the United States shall be composed of two Senators from each State, [chosen by the Legislature thereof,] for six Years; and each Senator shall have one Vote.

Immediately after they shall be assembled in Consequence of the first Election, they shall be divided as equally as may be into three Classes. The Seats of the Senators of the first Class shall be vacated at the Expiration of the second Year, of the second Class at the Expiration of the fourth Year, and of the third Class at the Expiration of the sixth Year, so that one-third may be chosen every second Year; [and if Vacancies happen by Resignation, or otherwise, during the Recess of the Legislature of any State, the Executive thereof may make temporary Appointments until the next Meeting of the Legislature, which shall then fill such Vacancies.]

No Person shall be a Senator who shall not have attained to the

Age of thirty Years, and been nine Years a Citizen of the United States, and who shall not, when elected, be an Inhabitant of that State for which he shall be chosen.

The Vice President of the United States shall be President of the Senate, but shall have no Vote, unless they be equally divided.

The Senate shall chuse their other Officers, and also a President pro tempore, in the absence of the Vice President, or when he shall exercise the Office of President of the United States.

The Senate shall have the sole Power to try all Impeachments. When sitting for that Purpose, they shall be on Oath or Affirmation. When the President of the United States is tried, the Chief Justice shall preside: And no Person shall be convicted without the Concurrence of two thirds of the Members present.

Judgment in Cases of Impeachment shall not extend further than to removal from Office, and disqualification to hold and enjoy any Office of honor, Trust or Profit under the United States: but the Party convicted shall nevertheless be liable and subject to Indictment, Trial, Judgment and Punishment, according to Law.

SECTION 4. The Times, Places and Manner of holding Elections for Senators and Representatives, shall be prescribed in each State by the Legislature thereof; but the Congress may at any time by Law make or alter such Regulations, except as to the Place of Chusing Senators.

The Congress shall assemble at least once in every Year, and such Meeting shall be on the first Monday in December, unless they shall by Law appoint a different Day.

SECTION 5. Each House shall be the Judge of the Elections, Returns and Qualifications of its own Members, and a Majority of each shall constitute a Quorum to do Business; but a smaller number may adjourn from day to day, and may be authorized to compel the Attendance of absent Members, in such Manner, and under such Penalties as each House may provide.

Each House may determine the Rules of its Proceedings, punish its Members for disorderly Behavior, and, with the Concurrence of two thirds, expel a Member.

Each House shall keep a Journal of its Proceedings, and from time to time publish the same, excepting such Parts as may in their Judgment require Secrecy; and the Yeas and Nays of the

Members of either House on any question shall, at the Desire of one fifth of those Present, be entered on the Journal.

Neither House, during the Session of Congress, shall, without the Consent of the other, adjourn for more than three days, nor to any other Place than that in which the two Houses shall be sitting.

SECTION 6. The Senators and Representatives shall receive a Compensation for their Services, to be ascertained by Law, and paid out of the Treasury of the United States. They shall in all Cases, except Treason, Felony and Breach of the Peace, be privileged from Arrest during their Attendance at the Session of their respective Houses, and in going to and returning from the same; and for any Speech or Debate in either House, they shall not be questioned in any other Place.

No Senator or Representative shall, during the Time for which he was elected, be appointed to any civil Office under the Authority of the United States, which shall have been created, or the Emoluments whereof shall have been encreased during such time; and no Person holding any Office under the United States, shall be a Member of either House during his Continuance in Office.

SECTION 7. All Bills for raising Revenue shall originate in the House of Representatives; but the Senate may propose or concur with Amendments as on other Bills.

Every Bill which shall have passed the House of Representatives and the Senate, shall, before it become a Law, be presented to the President of the United States; If he approve he shall sign it, but if not he shall return it, with his Objections to that House in which it shall have originated, who shall enter the Objections at large on their Journal, and proceed to reconsider it. If after such Reconsideration two thirds of that House shall agree to pass the Bill, it shall be sent, together with the Objections, to the other House, by which it shall likewise be reconsidered, and if approved by two thirds of that House, it shall become a Law. But in all such Cases the Votes of both Houses shall be determined by Yeas and Nays, and the Names of the Persons voting for and against the Bill shall be entered on the Journal of each House respectively. If any Bill shall not be returned by the President within ten Days (Sundays excepted) after it shall have been presented to him, the

Same shall be a Law, in like Manner as if he had signed it, unless the Congress by their Adjournment prevent its Return, in which Case it shall not be a Law.

Every Order, Resolution, or Vote to which the Concurrence of the Senate and House of Representatives may be necessary (except on a question of Adjournment) shall be presented to the President of the United States; and before the Same shall take Effect, shall be approved by him, or being disapproved by him, shall be repassed by two thirds of the Senate and House of Representatives, according to the Rules and Limitations prescribed in the Case of a Bill.

SECTION 8. The Congress shall have Power To lay and collect Taxes, Duties, Imposts and Excises, to pay the Debts and provide for the common Defence and general Welfare of the United States; but all Duties, Imposts and Excises shall be uniform throughout the United States;

To borrow money on the credit of the United States;

To regulate Commerce with foreign Nations, and among the several States, and with the Indian Tribes;

To establish an uniform Rule of Naturalization, and uniform Laws on the subject of Bankruptcies throughout the United States;

To coin Money, regulate the Value thereof, and of foreign Coin, and fix the Standard of Weights and Measures;

To provide for the Punishment of counterfeiting the Securities and current Coin of the United States;

To establish Post Offices and post Roads;

To promote the Progress of Science and useful Arts, by securing for limited Times to Authors and Inventors the exclusive Right to their respective Writings and Discoveries;

To constitute Tribunals inferior to the supreme Court;

To define and punish Piracies and Felonies committed on the high Seas, and Offenses against the Law of Nations;

To declare War, grant Letters of Marque and Reprisal, and make Rules concerning Captures on Land and Water;

To raise and support Armies, but no Appropriation of Money to that Use shall be for a longer Term than two Years;

To provide and maintain a Navy;

To make Rules for the Government and Regulation of the land and naval Forces;

To provide for calling forth the Militia to execute the Laws of the Union, suppress Insurrections and repel Invasions;

To provide for organizing, arming, and disciplining the Militia, and for governing such Part of them as may be employed in the Service of the United States, reserving to the States respectively, the Appointment of the Officers, and the Authority of training the Militia according to the discipline prescribed by Congress;

To exercise exclusive Legislation in all Cases whatsoever, over such District (not exceeding ten Miles square) as may, by Cession of particular States, and the acceptance of Congress, become the Seat of the Government of the United States, and to exercise like Authority over all Places purchased by the Consent of the Legislature of the State in which the Same shall be, for the Erection of Forts, Magazines, Arsenals, dock-Yards, and other needful Buildings;—And

To make all Laws which shall be necessary and proper for carrying into Execution the foregoing Powers, and all other Powers vested by this Constitution in the Government of the United States, or in any Department or Officer thereof.

SECTION 9. The Migration or Importation of such Persons as any of the States now existing shall think proper to admit, shall not be prohibited by the Congress prior to the Year one thousand eight hundred and eight, but a tax or duty may be imposed on such Importation, not exceeding ten dollars for each Person.

The privilege of the Writ of Habeas Corpus shall not be suspended, unless when in Cases of Rebellion or Invasion the public Safety may require it.

No Bill of Attainder or ex post facto Law shall be passed.

No capitation, or other direct, Tax shall be laid, unless in Proportion to the Census or Enumeration herein before directed to be taken.

No Tax or Duty shall be laid on Articles exported from any State.

No Preference shall be given by any Regulation of Commerce or Revenue to the Ports of one State over those of another: nor shall Vessels bound to, or from, one State, be obliged to enter, clear, or pay Duties in another.

No Money shall be drawn from the Treasury, but in Consequence of Appropriations made by Law; and a regular Statement and Account of the Receipts and Expenditures of all public Money shall be published from time to time.

No Title of Nobility shall be granted by the United States: And no Person holding any Office of Profit or Trust under them, shall, without the Consent of the Congress, accept of any present, Emolument, Office, or Title, of any kind whatever, from any King, Prince, or foreign State.

SECTION 10. No State shall enter into any Treaty, Alliance, or Confederation; grant Letters of Marque and Reprisal; coin Money; emit Bills of Credit; make any Thing but gold and silver Coin a Tender in Payment of Debts; pass any Bill of Attainder, ex post facto Law, or Law impairing the Obligation of Contracts, or grant any Title of Nobility.

No State shall, without the Consent of the Congress, lay any Imposts or Duties on Imports or Exports, except what may be absolutely necessary for executing its inspection Laws: and the net produce of all Duties and Imposts, laid by any State on Imports or Exports, shall be for the Use of the Treasury of the United States; and all such Laws shall be subject to the Revision and Controul of the Congress.

No state shall, without the Consent of Congress, lay any duty of Tonnage, keep Troops, or Ships of War in time of Peace, enter into any Agreement or Compact with another State, or with a foreign Power, or engage in War, unless actually invaded, or in such imminent Danger as will not admit of delay.

ARTICLE II.

SECTION 1. The executive Power shall be vested in a President of the United States of America. He shall hold his Office during the Term of four Years, and together with the Vice-President, chosen for the same Term, be elected, as follows.

Each State shall appoint, in such Manner as the Legislature thereof may direct, a Number of Electors, equal to the whole Number of Senators and Representatives to which the State may be entitled in the Congress: but no Senator or Representative, or Person holding an Office of Trust or Profit under the United States, shall be appointed an Elector.

The Electors shall meet in their respective States, and vote by

Ballot for two persons, of whom one at least shall not be an Inhabitant of the same State with themselves. And they shall make a List of all the Persons voted for, and of the Number of Votes for each; which List they shall sign and certify, and transmit sealed to the Seat of the Government of the United States, directed to the President of the Senate. The President of the Senate shall, in the Presence of the Senate and House of Representatives, open all the Certificates, and the Votes shall then be counted. The Person having the greatest Number of Votes shall be the President, if such Number be a Majority of the whole Number of Electors appointed; and if there be more than one who have such Majority, and have an equal Number of Votes, then the House of Representatives shall immediately chuse by Ballot one of them for President; and if no Person have a Majority, then from the five highest on the List the said House shall in like Manner chuse the President. But in chusing the President, the Votes shall be taken by States, the Representation from each State having one Vote; a quorum for this Purpose shall consist of a Member or Members from two thirds of the States, and a Majority of all the States shall be necessary to a Choice. In every Case, after the Choice of the President, the Person having the greatest Number of Votes of the Electors shall be the Vice President. But if there should remain two or more who have equal Votes, the Senate shall chuse from them by Ballot the Vice-President.

The Congress may determine the Time of chusing the Electors, and the Day on which they shall give their Votes; which Day shall be the same throughout the United States.

No person except a natural born Citizen, or a Citizen of the United States, at the time of the Adoption of this Constitution, shall be eligible to the Office of President; neither shall any Person be eligible to that Office who shall not have attained to the Age of thirty-five Years, and been fourteen Years a Resident within the United States.

In Case of the Removal of the President from Office, or of his Death, Resignation, or Inability to discharge the Powers and Duties of the said Office, the same shall devolve on the Vice President, and the Congress may by Law, provide for the Case of Removal, Death, Resignation or Inability, both of the President and Vice President, declaring what Officer shall then act as President, and such Officer shall act accordingly, until the Disability be removed, or a President shall be elected.

The President shall, at stated Times, receive for his Services, a Compensation, which shall neither be encreased nor diminished during the Period for which he shall have been elected, and he shall not receive within that Period any other Emolument from the United States, or any of them.

Before he enter on the Execution of his Office, he shall take the following Oath or Affirmation:—"I do solemnly swear (or affirm) that I will faithfully execute the Office of President of the United States, and will to the best of my Ability, preserve, protect and defend the Constitution of the United States."

SECTION 2. The President shall be Commander in Chief of the Army and Navy of the United States, and of the Militia of the several States, when called into the actual Service of the United States; he may require the Opinion in writing, of the principal Officer in each of the executive Departments, upon any subject relating to the Duties of their respective Offices, and he shall have Power to Grant Reprieves and Pardons for Offenses against the United States, except in Cases of Impeachment.

He shall have Power, by and with the Advice and Consent of the Senate, to make Treaties, provided two-thirds of the Senators present concur; and he shall nominate, and by and with the Advice and Consent of the Senate, shall appoint Ambassadors, other public Ministers and Consuls, Judges of the supreme Court, and all other Officers of the United States, whose Appointments are not herein otherwise provided for, and which shall be established by Law: but the Congress may by Law vest the Appointment of such inferior Officers, as they think proper, in the President alone, in the Courts of Law, or in the Heads of Departments.

The President shall have Power to fill up all Vacancies that may happen during the Recess of the Senate, by granting Commissions which shall expire at the End of their next Session.

SECTION 3. He shall from time to time give to the Congress Information of the State of the Union, and recommend to their Consideration such Measures as he shall judge necessary and expedient; he may, on extraordinary Occasions, convene both Houses, or either of them, and in Case of Disagreement between them, with Respect to the Time of Adjournment, he may adjourn them to such Time as he shall think proper; he shall receive Ambassadors and other public Ministers; he shall take Care that the Laws be faithfully executed, and shall Commission all the Officers of the United States.

SECTION 4. The President, Vice President and all civil Officers of the United States, shall be removed from Office on Impeachment for, and Conviction of, Treason, Bribery, or other high Crimes and Misdemeanors.

### ARTICLE III.

SECTION 1. The judicial Power of the United States, shall be vested in one supreme Court, and in such inferior Courts as the Congress may from time to time ordain and establish. The Judges, both of the supreme and inferior Courts, shall hold their Offices during good Behaviour, and shall, at stated Times, receive for their Services, a Compensation, which shall not be diminished during their Continuance in Office.

SECTION 2. The judicial Power shall extend to all Cases, in Law and Equity, arising under this Constitution, the Laws of the United States, and Treaties made, or which shall be made, under their Authority;—to all Cases affecting Ambassadors, other public Ministers and Consuls;—to all Cases of admiralty and maritime Jurisdiction;—to Controversies to which the United States shall be a Party;—to Controversies between two or more States;—between a State and Citizens of another State;—between Citizens of different States;—between Citizens of the same State claiming Lands under Grants of different States, and between a State, or the Citizens thereof, and foreign States, Citizens or Subjects.

In all Cases affecting Ambassadors, other public Ministers and Consuls, and those in which a State shall be party, the supreme Court shall have original Jurisdiction. In all the other Cases before mentioned, the supreme Court shall have appellate Jurisdiction, both as to Law and Fact, with such Exceptions, and under such Regulations as the Congress shall make.

The trial of all Crimes, except in Cases of Impeachment, shall be by Jury; and such Trial shall be held in the State where the said Crimes shall have been committed; but when not committed within any State, the Trial shall be at such Place or Places as the Congress may by Law have directed.

SECTION 3. Treason against the United States, shall consist only in levying War against them, or in adhering to their Enemies, giving them Aid and Comfort. No Person shall be convicted of Treason unless on the Testimony of two Witnesses to the same overt Act, or on Confession in open Court.

The Congress shall have Power to declare the Punishment of Treason, but no Attainder of Treason shall work Corruption of Blood, or Forfeiture except during the Life of the Person attainted.

ARTICLE IV.

SECTION 1. Full Faith and Credit shall be given in each State to the public Acts, Records, and judicial Proceedings of every other State. And the Congress may by general Laws prescribe the Manner in which such Acts, Records and Proceedings shall be proved, and the Effect thereof.

SECTION 2. The Citizens of each State shall be entitled to all Privileges and Immunities of Citizens in the several States.

A Person charged in any State with Treason, Felony, or other Crime, who shall flee from Justice, and be found in another State, shall on demand of the executive Authority of the State from which he fled, be delivered up, to be removed to the State having Jurisdiction of the Crime.

No Person held to Service or Labour in one State, under the Laws thereof, escaping into another, shall, in Consequence of any Law or Regulation therein, be discharged from such Service or Labour, but shall be delivered up on Claim of the Party to whom such Service or Labour may be due.

SECTION 3. New States may be admitted by the Congress into this Union; but no new State shall be formed or erected within the Jurisdiction of any other State; nor any State be formed by the Junction of two or more States, or parts of States, without the Consent of the Legislatures of the States concerned as well as of the Congress.

The Congress shall have Power to dispose of and make all needful Rules and Regulations respecting the Territory or other Property belonging to the United States; and nothing in this Constitution shall be so construed as to Prejudice any Claims of The United States, or of any particular State.

SECTION 4. The United States shall guarantee to every State in this Union a Republican Form of Government, and shall protect each of them against Invasion; and on Application of the Legislature, or of the Executive (when the Legislature cannot be convened) against domestic Violence.

ARTICLE V.

The Congress, whenever two-thirds of both Houses shall deem it necessary, shall propose Amendments to this Constitution, or, on the Application of the Legislatures of two-thirds of the several States, shall call a Convention for proposing Amendments, which, in either Case, shall be valid to all Intents and Purposes, as part of this Constitution, when ratified by the Legislatures of three-fourths of the several States, or by Conventions in three-fourths thereof, as the one or the other Mode of Ratification may be proposed by the Congress: Provided that no Amendment which may be made prior to the Year One thousand eight hundred and eight shall in any Manner affect the first and fourth Clauses in the Ninth Section of the first Article; and that no State without its Consent, shall be deprived of its equal Suffrage in the Senate.

ARTICLE VI.

All Debts contracted and Engagements entered into, before the Adoption of this Constitution, shall be as valid against the United States under this Constitution, as under the Confederation.

This Constitution, and the Laws of the United States which shall be made in Pursuance thereof; and all Treaties made, or which shall be made, under the Authority of the United States, shall be the supreme Law of the Land; and the Judges in every State shall be bound thereby, any Thing in the Constitution or Laws of any State to the Contrary notwithstanding.

The Senators and Representatives before mentioned, and the Members of the several State Legislatures, and all executive and judicial Officers, both of the United States and of the several States, shall be bound by Oath or Affirmation, to support this Constitution; but no religious Test shall ever be required as a Qualification to any Office or public Trust under the United States.

### ARTICLE VII.

The Ratification of the Conventions of nine States shall be sufficient for the Establishment of this Constitution between the States so ratifying the Same.

DONE in Convention by the Unanimous Consent of the States present in the Seventeenth Day of September in the Year of our Lord one thousand seven hundred and Eighty seven and of the Independence of the United States of America the Twelfth.

In Witness whereof We have hereunto subscribed our Names.

*Go WASHINGTON*
*Presidt and deputy from Virginia*

*New Hampshire.*

JOHN LANGDON
NICHOLAS GILMAN

*Massachusetts.*

NATHANIEL GORHAM
RUFUS KING

*New Jersey.*

WIL: LIVINGSTON
DAVID BREARLEY.
WM PATERSON.
JONA: DAYTON

*Pennsylvania.*

B FRANKLIN
ROBT. MORRIS
THOS. FITZSIMONS
JAMES WILSON
THOMAS MIFFLIN
GEO. CLYMER
JARED INGERSOLL
GOUV MORRIS

*Delaware.*

GEO: READ
JOHN DICKINSON
JACO: BROOM

GUNNING BEDFORD jun
RICHARD BASSETT

*Connecticut.*

WM. SAML JOHNSON
ROGER SHERMAN

*New York.*

ALEXANDER HAMILTON

*Maryland.*

JAMES MCHENRY
DANL CARROL
DAN: of ST THOS JENIFER

*Virginia.*

JOHN BLAIR
JAMES MADISON JR.

*North Carolina.*

WM BLOUNT
HU WILLIAMSON
RICHD DOBBS SPAIGHT.

*South Carolina.*

J. RUTLEDGE
CHARLES PINCKNEY
CHARLES COTESWORTH
PINCKNEY
PIERCE BUTLER

*Georgia.*

WILLIAM FEW
ABR BALDWIN

Attest:

*WILLIAM JACKSON, Secretary.*

[*The first ten amendments were proposed September 25, 1789, and ratified December 15, 1791. They form what is known as the Bill of Rights.*]

AMENDMENT I

Congress shall make no law respecting an establishment of religion, or prohibiting the free exercise thereof; or abridging the freedom of speech, or of the press; or the right of the people peaceably to assemble, and to petition the Government for a redress of grievances.

118

### AMENDMENT II

A well regulated Militia, being necessary to the security of a free State, the right of the people to keep and bear Arms, shall not be infringed.

### AMENDMENT III

No Soldier shall, in time of peace be quartered in any house, without the consent of the Owner, nor in time of war, but in a manner to be prescribed by law.

### AMENDMENT IV

The right of the people to be secure in their persons, houses, papers, and effects, against unreasonable searches and seizures, shall not be violated, and no Warrants shall issue, but upon probable cause, supported by Oath or affirmation, and particularly describing the place to be searched, and the persons or things to be seized.

### AMENDMENT V

No person shall be held to answer for a capital, or otherwise infamous crime, unless on a presentment or indictment of a Grand Jury, except in cases arising in the land or naval forces, or in the Militia, when in actual service in time of War or public danger; nor shall any person be subject for the same offence to be twice put in jeopardy of life or limb; nor shall be compelled in any criminal case to be a witness against himself, nor be deprived of life, liberty, or property, without due process of law; nor shall private property be taken for public use, without just compensation.

### AMENDMENT VI

In all criminal prosecutions, the accused shall enjoy the right to a speedy and public trial, by an impartial jury of the State and district herein the crime shall have been committed, which district shall have been previously ascertained by law, and to be informed of the nature and cause of the accusation; to be confronted with the witnesses against him; to have compulsory process for obtaining witnesses in his favor, and to have the Assistance of Counsel for his defence.

### AMENDMENT VII

In suits at common law, where the value in controversy shall exceed twenty dollars, the right of trial by jury shall be preserved, and no fact tried by a jury, shall be otherwise reexamined in any Court of the United States, than according to the rules of the common law.

### AMENDMENT VIII

Excessive bail shall not be required, nor excessive fines imposed, nor cruel and unusual punishments inflicted.

### AMENDMENT IX

The enumeration in the Constitution, of certain rights, shall not be construed to deny or disparage others retained by the people.

### AMENDMENT X

The powers not delegated to the United States by the Constitution, nor prohibited by it to the States, are reserved to the States respectively, or to the people.

### AMENDMENT XI
[*Proposed March 5, 1794; ratified February 7, 1795*]

The Judicial power of the United States shall not be construed to extend to any suit in law or equity, commenced or prosecuted against one of the United States by Citizens of another State, or by Citizens or Subjects of any Foreign State.

## AMENDMENT XII

*[Proposed December 12, 1803; ratified June 15, 1804]*

The Electors shall meet in their respective states and vote by ballot for President and Vice-President, one of whom, at least, shall not be an inhabitant of the same state with themselves; they shall name in their ballots the person voted for as President, and in distinct ballots the person voted for as Vice-President, and they shall make distinct lists of all persons voted for as President, and of all persons voted for as Vice-President, and of the number of votes for each, which lists they shall sign and certify, and transmit sealed to the seat of the government of the United States, directed to the President of the Senate;—The President of the Senate shall, in presence of the Senate and House of Representatives, open all the certificates and the votes shall then be counted;—The person having the greatest number of votes for President, shall be the President, if such number be a majority of the whole number of Electors appointed; and if no person have such majority, then from the persons having the highest numbers not exceeding three on the list of those voted for as President, the House of Representatives shall choose immediately, by ballot, the President. But in choosing the President, the votes shall be taken by states, the representation from each state having one vote; a quorum for this purpose shall consist of a member or members from two-thirds of the states, and a majority of all the states shall be necessary to a choice. And if the House of Representatives shall not choose a President whenever the right of choice shall devolve upon them, before the fourth day of March next following, then the Vice-President shall act as President, as in the case of the death or other constitutional disability of the President.—The person having the greatest number of votes as Vice-President, shall be the Vice President if such number be a majority of the whole number of Electors appointed, and if no person have a majority, then from the two highest numbers on the list, the Senate shall choose the Vice-President; a quorum for the purpose shall consist of two-thirds of the whole number of Senators, and a majority of the whole number shall be necessary to a choice. But no person constitutionally ineligible to the office of President shall be eligible to that of Vice-President of the United States.

AMENDMENT XIII
*[Proposed February 1, 1865; ratified December 6, 1865]*

SECTION 1. Neither slavery nor involuntary servitude, except as a punishment for crime whereof the party shall have been duly convicted, shall exist within the United States, or any place subject to their jurisdiction.

SECTION 2. Congress shall have power to enforce this article by appropriate legislation.

AMENDMENT XIV
*[Proposed June 16, 1866; ratified July 9, 1868]*

SECTION 1. All persons born or naturalized in the United States, and subject to the jurisdiction thereof, are citizens of the United States and of the State wherein they reside. No State shall make or enforce any law which shall abridge the privileges or immunities of citizens of the United States; nor shall any State deprive any person of life, liberty, or property, without due process of law; nor deny to any person within its jurisdiction the equal protection of the laws.

SECTION 2. Representatives shall be apportioned among the several States according to their respective numbers, counting the whole number of persons in each State, excluding Indians not taxed. But when the right to vote at any election for the choice of electors for President and Vice-President of the United States, Representatives in Congress, the Executive and Judicial officers of a State, or the members of the Legislature thereof, is denied to any of the male inhabitants of such State, being twenty-one years of age, and citizens of the United States, or in any way abridged, except for participation in rebellion, or other crime, the basis of representation therein shall be reduced in the proportion which the number of such male citizens shall bear to the whole number of male citizens twenty-one years of age in such State.

SECTION 3. No person shall be a Senator or Representative in Congress, or elector of President and Vice-President, or hold any office, civil or military, under the United States, or under any State, who, having previously taken an oath, as a member of Congress, or as an officer of the United States, or as a member of any State legislature, or as an executive or judicial officer of any State, to support the Constitution of the United States, shall have engaged in insurrection or rebellion against the same, or given aid or comfort to the enemies thereof. But Congress may by a vote of two-thirds of each House, remove such disability.

SECTION 4. The validity of the public debt of the United States, authorized by law, including debts incurred for payment of pensions and bounties for services in suppressing insurrection or rebellion, shall not be questioned. But neither the United States nor any State shall assume or pay any debt or obligation incurred in aid of insurrection or rebellion against the United States, or any claim for the loss or emancipation of any slave; but all such debts, obligations and claims shall be held illegal and void.

SECTION 5. The Congress shall have power to enforce, by appropriate legislation, the provisions of this article.

## AMENDMENT XV
*[Proposed February 27, 1869; ratified February 3, 1870]*

SECTION 1. The right of citizens of the United States to vote shall not be denied or abridged by the United States or by any State on account of race, color, or previous conditions of servitude—

SECTION 2. The Congress shall have power to enforce this article by appropriate legislation.

## AMENDMENT XVI
*[Proposed July 12, 1909; ratified February 3, 1913]*

The Congress shall have power to lay and collect taxes on incomes, from whatever source derived, without apportionment among the several States, and without regard to any census or enumeration.

## AMENDMENT XVII
*[Proposed May 16, 1912; ratified April 8, 1913]*

The Senate of the United States shall be composed of two Senators from each State, elected by the people thereof, for six years;

and each Senator shall have one vote. The electors in each State shall have the qualifications requisite for electors of the most numerous branch of the State legislatures.

When vacancies happen in the representation of any State in the Senate, the executive authority of such State shall issue writs of election to fill such vacancies: *Provided,* That the legislature of any State may empower the executive thereof to make temporary appointments until the people fill the vacancies by election as the legislature may direct.

This amendment shall not be so construed as to affect the election or term of any Senator chosen before it becomes valid as part of the Constitution.

### AMENDMENT XVIII

*[Proposed December 18, 1917; ratified January 16, 1919; repealed December 5, 1933]*

SECTION 1. After one year from the ratification of this article the manufacture, sale, or transportation of intoxicating liquors within, the importation thereof into, or the exportation thereof from the United States and all territory subject to the jurisdiction thereof for beverage purposes is hereby prohibited.

SECTION 2. The Congress and the several States shall have concurrent power to enforce this article by appropriate legislation.

SECTION 3. This article shall be inoperative unless it shall have been ratified as an amendment to the Constitution by the legislatures of the several States as provided in the Constitution, within seven years from the date of the submission hereof to the States by the Congress.

### AMENDMENT XIX

*[Proposed June 4, 1919; ratified August 18, 1920]*

The right of citizens of the United States to vote shall not be denied or abridged by the United States or by any State on account of sex.

Congress shall have power to enforce this article by appropriate legislation.

AMENDMENT XX
[*Proposed March 2, 1932; ratified January 23, 1933*]

SECTION 1. The terms of the President and Vice President shall end at noon on the 20th day of January, and the terms of Senators and Representatives at noon on the 3rd day of January, of the years in which such terms would have ended if this article had not been ratified; and the terms of their successors shall then begin.

SECTION 2. The Congress shall assemble at least once in every year, and such meeting shall begin at noon on the 3d day of January, unless they shall by law appoint a different day.

SECTION 3. If, at the time fixed for the beginning of the term of the President, the President elect shall have died, the Vice President elect shall become President. If a President shall not have been chosen before the time fixed for the beginning of his term, or if the President elect shall have failed to qualify, then the Vice President elect shall act as President until a President shall have qualified; and the Congress may by law provide for the case wherein neither a President elect nor a Vice President elect shall have qualified, declaring who shall then act as President, or the manner in which one who is to act shall be selected, and such person shall act accordingly until a President or Vice President shall have qualified.

SECTION 4. The Congress may by law provide for the case of the death of any of the persons from whom the House of Representatives may choose a President whenever the right of choice shall have devolved upon them, and for the case of the death of any of the persons from whom the Senate may choose a Vice President whenever the right of choice shall have devolved upon them.

SECTION 5. Sections 1 and 2 shall take effect on the 15th day of October following the ratification of this article.

SECTION 6. This article shall be inoperative unless it shall have been ratified as an amendment to the Constitution by the legislatures of three-fourths of the several States within seven years from the date of its submission.

AMENDMENT XXI

[*Proposed February 20, 1933; ratified December 5, 1933*]

SECTION 1. The eighteenth article of amendment to the Constitution of the United States is hereby repealed.

SECTION 2. The transportation or importation into any State, Territory, or possession of the United States for delivery or use therein of intoxicating liquors, in violation of the laws thereof, is hereby prohibited.

SECTION 3. This article shall be inoperative unless it shall have been ratified as an amendment to the Constitution by conventions in the several States, as provided in the Constitution, within seven years from the date of the submission hereof to the States by the Congress.

AMENDMENT XXII

[*Proposed March 24, 1947; ratified February 27, 1951*]

SECTION 1. No person shall be elected to the office of the President more than twice, and no person who has held the office of President, or acted as President, for more than two years of a term to which some other person was elected President shall be elected to the office of the President more than once. But this Article shall not apply to any person holding the office of President when this Article was proposed by the Congress, and shall not prevent any person who may be holding the office of President, or acting as President, during the term within which this Article becomes operative from holding the office of President or acting as President during the remainder of such term.

SECTION 2. This article shall be inoperative unless it shall have been ratified as an amendment to the Constitution by the legislatures of three-fourths of the several States within seven years from the date of its submission to the States by the Congress.

AMENDMENT XXIII

[*Proposed June 16, 1960; ratified March 29, 1961*]

SECTION 1. The District constituting the seat of Government of the United States shall appoint in such manner as the Congress may direct:

A number of electors of President and Vice President equal to the whole number of Senators and Representatives in Congress to which the District would be entitled if it were a State, but in no event more than the least populous State; they shall be in addition to those appointed by the States, but they shall be considered, for the purposes of the election of President and Vice President, to be electors appointed by a State; and they shall meet in the District and perform such duties as provided by the twelfth article of amendment.

SECTION 2. The Congress shall have power to enforce this article by appropriate legislation.

## AMENDMENT XXIV
### [Proposed August 27, 1962; ratified January 23, 1964]

SECTION 1. The right of citizens of the United States to vote in any primary or other election for President or Vice President, for electors for President or Vice President, or for Senator or Representative in Congress, shall not be denied or abridged by the United States or any State by reason of failure to pay any poll tax or other tax.

SECTION 2. The Congress shall have power to enforce this article by appropriate legislation.

## AMENDMENT XXV
### [Proposed July 6, 1965; ratified February 10, 1967]

SECTION 1. In case of the removal of the President from office or of his death or resignation, the Vice President shall become President.

SECTION 2. Whenever there is a vacancy in the office of the Vice President, the President shall nominate a Vice President who shall take office upon confirmation by a majority vote of both Houses of Congress.

SECTION 3. Whenever the President transmits to the President pro tempore of the Senate and the Speaker of the House of Representatives his written declaration that he is unable to discharge the powers and duties of his office, and until he transmits to them a written declaration to the contrary, such powers and duties shall be discharged by the Vice President as Acting President.

SECTION 4. Whenever the Vice President and a majority of either the principal officers of the executive departments or of such other body as Congress may by law provide, transmit to the President pro tempore of the Senate and the Speaker of the House of Representatives their written declaration that the President is unable to discharge the powers and duties of his office, the Vice President shall immediately assume the powers and duties of the office as Acting President.

Thereafter, when the President transmits to the President pro tempore of the Senate and the Speaker of the House of Representatives his written declaration that no inability exists, he shall resume the powers and duties of his office unless the Vice President and a majority of either the principal officers of the executive department or of such other body as Congress may by law provide, transmit within four days to the President pro tempore of the Senate and the Speaker of the House of Representatives their written declaration that the President is unable to discharge the powers and duties of his office. Thereupon Congress shall decide the issue, assembling within forty-eight hours for that purpose if not in session. If the Congress, within twenty-one days after receipt of the latter written declaration, or, if Congress is not in session, within twenty-one days after Congress is required to assemble, determines by two-thirds vote of both Houses that the President is unable to discharge the powers and duties of his office, the Vice President shall continue to discharge the same as Acting President; otherwise the President shall resume the powers and duties of his office.

AMENDMENT XXVI
[*Proposed March 23, 1971; ratified July 1, 1971*]

SECTION 1. The right of citizens of the United States, who are eighteen years of age or older, to vote shall not be denied or abridged by the United States or by any State on account of age.

SECTION 2. The Congress shall have power to enforce this article by appropriate legislation.

# GLOSSARY

**Act**   A formal legislative decision or law

**Amendment**   An alteration of or addition to a document

**Antifederalist**   One who opposed ratification of the Constitution and, later, favored a weak national government and strong state governments

**Article**   In the Constitution, the larger units of which the document is composed

**Bill**   Draft of a statute being considered by a legislature but not yet enacted

**Bill of attainder**   A legislative act by which an individual is stripped of rights or property

**Bill of Rights**   In the Constitution of the United States, the first ten amendments, outlining basic individual rights that the federal government may not abridge

**Civil rights**   Legal, economic, and social rights

**Committee of the whole house**   A parliamentary device, particularly useful as a means of ascertaining the sense of a meeting, that allows for debate free of the usual strictures and for nonbinding votes

**Confederation**   An association of sovereign states

**Constitution**   A document outlining the powers granted to a government and describing how and by whom those powers are to be exercised

**Due process**   The legal proceedings required before an individual can be deprived of life, liberty, or property

**Elector**   One person chosen as the representative of many in the voting for the president

**Engross**   To copy on parchment in fine clerk's script

**Ex post facto law**   A law that punishes deeds not illegal prior to enactment of the law

**Executive**   The branch of the government that carries out the decisions made by the legislature

**Extraordinary majority**   Votes totaling well over half of all that are cast

**Federalism**   The division of powers into separate systems—that of the national government and that of the state governments

**Federalist**   One who favored the Constitution and, later, a strong national government

**Framers**   Referring to the framing, or outlining, of the Constitution, a term for the delegates to the Federal Convention

**Grand jury**   A jury that determines if there is enough evidence that a crime has been committed to hold a trial

**Impeachment**   The accusation and trial of a public official for misconduct in office

**Impost**   A tax on goods moving from one state into or through another

**Incorporation**   The process by which states, as well as the federal government, are required to respect most of the protections guaranteed by the Bill of Rights

**Judicial review**   The judicial branch's power to scrutinize legislative acts and executive actions and to void those that are deemed unconstitutional

**Judiciary**   The branch of the government that operates courts of justice

**Jurisdiction**   The power of the judiciary to hear and rule on a case

**Legislature**   The branch of the government that enacts laws

**Negative**   The term used by the framers for veto

**Precedent**   *See* **stare decisis**

**Quorum**   The number of members of a body required to be in attendance for the group to conduct business

**Ratify**   To confirm formally something arranged by a representative

**Repeal**   To revoke or annul officially

**Republic**   A government in which representatives of the people make laws and put them into effect

**Sovereignty**   The supreme authority to make and carry out decisions

**Stare decisis**   Literally "to adhere to decided cases," the policy of basing current judicial decisions on past decisions so that the body of law is cohesive and consistent

**Suffrage**   The right to vote

**Tribunal**   A court of justice

**Writ of habeas corpus**   The mechanism by which a person can test the legality of his or her detention

# NOTES

## Chapter 1

1. Catherine Drinker Bowen, *Miracle at Philadelphia: The Story of the Constitutional Convention, May to September 1787* (Boston: Atlantic Monthly Press/Little, Brown and Company, 1966), p. 9.
2. Charles A. Beard, *An Economic Interpretation of the Constitution of the United States* (New York: Free Press, Macmillan Publishing Co., 1935), p. 33.
3. Page Smith, *The Constitution: A Documentary and Narrative History* (New York: William Morrow and Co., 1978), p. 87.
4. Carl Van Doren, *The Great Rehearsal* (New York: Viking Press, 1948), p. 7.
5. Max Farrand, ed., *The Records of the Federal Convention of 1787*, revised edition, 4 vols. (New Haven: Yale University Press, 1937), 3: 14.

## Chapter 2

1. Bowen, *Miracle at Philadelphia*, p. 4.
2. *Records of the Federal Convention*, 3: 550.
3. Ibid., 1: 30.
4. Ibid., 1: 301.
5. Ibid., 1: 438.
6. Bowen, *Miracle at Philadelphia*, p. 127.

7. *Records of the Federal Convention*, 1: 486–87.

## Chapter 3

1. *Records of the Federal Convention*, 1: 532.
2. Ibid., 2: 249.
3. Ibid., 3: 74.
4. Ibid., 2: 631.
5. Ibid., 2: 632–33.
6. Ibid., 2: 642–43.
7. Ibid., 2: 648.

## Chapter 4

1. Bowen, *Miracle at Philadelphia*, p. 301.
2. Beard, *An Economic Interpretation*, p. 299.

## Chapter 5

1. Bowen, *Miracle at Philadelphia*, p. 246.
2. Alpheus Thomas Mason, *The States Rights Debate: Antifederalism and the Constitution* (Englewood Cliffs, N.J.: Spectrum Books, Prentice-Hall, 1964), p. 168.
3. Bernard Schwartz, *The Great Rights of Mankind: A History of the American Bill of Rights* (New York: Oxford University Press, 1977), p. 6.
4. Ibid.
5. Ibid., p. 177.
6. Ibid., pp. 186–87.
7. Ibid., p. 61.
8. Ibid., p. 178.

## Chapter 6

1. Janet K. Boles, "Systemic Factors Underlying Legislative Responses to Woman Suffrage and the Equal Rights Amendment," in *Women & Politics*, ed. Sarah Slavin, vol. 2, nos. 1–2, Spring/Summer 1982, p. 17.

2. Catharine Stimpson, ed., *Women and the "Equal Rights" Amendment: Senate Subcommittee Hearings of the Constitutional Amendment, 91st Congress* (New York: R. R. Bowker Company, 1972), p. xiv.

3. Susan S. Shear, "Introduction," in *Women & Politics*, p. 1.

## Chapter 7

1. Fred W. Friendly and Martha J. H. Elliott, *The Constitution: That Delicate Balance* (New York: Random House, 1984), pp. 9–10.

2. Henry Steele Commager, *Majority Rule and Minority Rights* (New York: Peter Smith, 1950), p. 34.

3. Beard, *An Economic Interpretation*, p. v.

4. Alexander M. Bickel, *The Supreme Court and the Idea of Progress* (New York: Harper & Row, 1970), p. 27.

## Chapter 8

1. Mason, *The States Rights Debate*, p. 169.

2. Ibid., p. 170.

3. Schwartz, *The Great Rights of Mankind*, p. 204.

4. Smith, *The Constitution: A Documentary and Narrative History*, p. 444.

5. Michi Weglyn, *Years of Infamy: The Untold Story of America's Concentration Camps* (New York: William Morrow and Co., 1976), p. 28.

6. Peter Irons, *Justice at War* (New York: Oxford University Press, 1983), p. viii.

7. Smith, *The Constitution: A Documentary and Narrative History*, pp. 433–34.

8. Ibid., pp. 361–62.

9. Friendly and Elliott, *The Constitution: That Delicate Balance*, p. 275.

10. *The Wounded Generation: America after Vietnam*, A. D. Horne, ed. (Englewood Cliffs, N.J.: Washington Post Books, Prentice-Hall, 1981), p. 5.

NOTES

11. Friendly and Elliott, *The Constitution: That Delicate Balance*, p. 205.
12. Ibid., p. 207.
13. Robert J. Steamer, *The Supreme Court in Crisis: A History of Conflict* (Amherst: University of Massachusetts Press, 1971), p. 150.

# BIBLIOGRAPHY

The genius of the framers and the remarkable longevity of the document they crafted are so stunning that no anniversary was needed to fill library shelves with books on the creation and evolution of our national government.

*The Records of the Federal Convention of 1787*, revised edition, 4 vols., edited by Max Farrand (New Haven: Yale University Press, 1937) brings together the formal minutes of the meetings and the notes kept by various delegates. It is the essential text for those interested in the formulation of the Constitution. A splendid book that chronicles the Federal Convention and ratification by the states is Carl Van Doren's *The Great Rehearsal* (New York: Viking Press, 1948). It is particularly valuable for its appendices. Van Doren's title expresses his hope that the American experience might serve as a model for all the world's nations to come together in a federation. Another book that describes the Federal Convention and ratification is *Miracle at Philadelphia: The Story of the Constitutional Convention,* by Catherine Drinker Bowen (Boston: Atlantic Monthly Press/Little, Brown and Company, 1966). Bowen's vivid descriptions of the framers and of the convention's drama have made her book a classic. In *The Constitution: A Documentary and Narrative History* (New York: William Morrow and Company, 1978), Page Smith describes the Federal Convention, with emphasis on eighteenth-century philosophical views, then turns his attention to the judiciary and how that branch's decisions have reflected and altered American thought on the individual and society over the last two hundred years. "The British Lose America," Barbara W. Tuchman's chapter on the events leading to the American Revolution in *The March of Folly: From Troy to Vietnam* (New York: Alfred A. Knopf, 1984), is useful in providing a sense of the British system of government and the institutional flaws that caused the war—flaws the framers were bent on minimizing when devising a national government. *The Articles of Confederation: An Interpretation of the Social-Constitutional History of the American Revolution, 1774–1781,* by Merrill Jensen (Madison, WI: University of Wisconsin Press, 1970), describes the process by which the Articles of Confederation and Perpetual Union were formulated. First published in 1913, *An Economic Interpretation of the Constitution of the United States,* by Charles A. Beard (New York: Free Press, Macmillan Publishing Company, 1935), is essential reading for those interested in the economic forces that gave rise to the Constitution. The eighty-five essays that make up *The Federalist,* by Alexander Hamilton, John Jay, and James Madison (New York: Modern Library/Random House, 1941), remain required reading for serious students of American government and government in general. Bernard Schwartz's *The Great Rights of Mankind: A History of the American Bill of Rights* (New York: Oxford University Press, 1977) is an excellent account of the Bill of Rights—its antecedents, its preparation and adoption, its service in protecting Americans' liberties. The historical background for the issue of states rights, as lively a topic today as it was in 1787, is considered by Alpheus Thomas Mason in *The States Rights Debate: Antifederalism and the Constitution* (Englewood Cliffs, NJ: Spectrum Books, Prentice-Hall, 1964). *The International Relations Dictionary,* by Jack C. Plano and Roy Olton (New York: Holt, Rinehart and Winston, 1969) is a valuable reference for those in search of extended definitions of words such as "democracy" and "natural law" and of descriptions of the way government is arranged in various countries.

*The Supreme Court in Crisis: A History of Conflict,* by Robert J. Steamer (Amherst: University of Massachusetts Press, 1971), is an excellent history of the Supreme Court and the crises that, Steamer believes, are inevitable because of the singular nature of this branch. *Majority Rule and Minority Rights,* by Henry Steele Commager (New York: Peter Smith, 1950), is a concise but provocative essay on the role of the courts. Charles A. Beard considers the framers' views on the judiciary and judicial review in *The Supreme Court and the Constitution* (Englewood Cliffs, NJ: Spectrum Books, Prentice-Hall, 1962). Two other books that consider judicial review are *Congress v. The Supreme Court,* by Raoul Berger (Cambridge, MA: Harvard University Press, 1969), and *Democracy and Distrust: A Theory of Judicial Review,* by John Hart Ely (Cambridge, MA: Harvard University Press, 1980). Raoul Berger looks at how the judiciary has applied the Fourteenth Amendment in *Government by Judiciary: The Transformation of the Fourteenth Amendment* (Cambridge, MA: Harvard University Press, 1977). *The Supreme Court and the Idea of Progress,* by Alexander M. Bickel (New York: Harper & Row, 1970), looks at decisions by the Warren court, particularly in the areas of reapportionment and school desegregation, but it requires a firm grounding in those issues. *The Constitution: That Delicate Balance,* by Fred W. Friendly and Martha J. H. Elliott (New York: Random House, 1984), is a wonderful book that looks at the human stories that gave rise to landmark decisions on issues as diverse as freedom of the press and reverse discrimination. *Freedom Spent,* by Richard Harris (Boston: Little, Brown and Company, 1976), is a collection of superb essays detailing three cases in which ordinary Americans were denied the freedoms guaranteed by the Bill of Rights by the very government that should protect those freedoms.

In *God Save this Honorable Court: How the Choice of Supreme Court Justices Shapes Our History,* by Laurence Tribe (New York: Random House, 1985), the reader will find an excellent, accessible discussion of the process by which Supreme Court justices are appointed and the importance of each individual appointment. A gossipy book that is valuable for its insider's view of how the Supreme Court works is Bob Woodward and Scott Armstrong's *The Brethren: Inside the Supreme Court* (New York: Simon and Schuster, 1979). Michael Kammen examines Americans' perception of the Constitution over the nearly two centuries since its writing in *A Machine That Would Go of Itself: The Constitution in American Culture* (New York: Alfred A. Knopf, 1986).

# INDEX

Abortion, 98–99
Accused, rights of, 62–63
Act, definition of, 129
Adams, John, 4, 91
Adams, Samuel, role in Massachusetts's ratification of Constitution, 45–47
Advice and consent, Senate's power of, 33, 35
Affirmative action, 99–100
Agnew, Spiro, 72
Amendment process, 73
  as check and balance to judiciary, 85–86
  for Constitution, provisions for, 35
  as outlined in Virginia Plan, 18
Amendments
  definition of, 129
  to Constitution. See U.S. Constitution, Amendments
  proposed by states during ratification, 45–52
  as basis of Bill of Rights, 58
American Revolution, 1–3
  war debt, 7
American Women's Suffrage Association, 70
Annapolis Convention, 9, 11
Anthony, Susan B., 70

Antifederalists, 101
  definition of, 129
  efforts opposing ratification, 47–48
    in Massachusetts, 45–46
    in Pennsylvania, 44–45
    in Virginia, 48
  opposition to Bill of Rights, 60
  opposition to Constitution, 43
  position on judiciary, 77–79
Article, definition of, 129
Articles of Confederation
  Article XIII, 30
  powers of, 4–5
  ratification of, 3–4
  states' relationships under, 4
  weakness of, 9

Bakke v. University of California, 100
Bill, definition of, 129
Bill of attainder, 53
  definition of, 129
Bill of Rights, 50, 51, 102. See also U.S. Constitution, Amendments
  Congress's debate on, 59–60
  Congress's passage of, 60
  criticism of Constitution for lacking, 43

# INDEX

# INDEX

Maryland
- delegates to Federal Convention, 23, 104
- delegates' vote on Virginia Plan, 22
- dispute with Virginia, during Confederation, 9
- opposition to Great Compromise, 30
- position on legislative representation, at Federal Convention, 28
- ratification of Constitution, 47

Mason, George, 48, 59
- criticism of Constitution's lack of bill of rights, 43
- at Federal Convention, 18, 37
- *Objections to the Constitution*, 41
- refusal to sign the Constitution, 39

Massachusetts. *See also* Shay's Rebellion
- claim to Western Territory, 7
- delegates to Federal Convention, 18, 103
- navigation acts, 6
- position on legislative representation, 4
- at Federal Convention, 28
- ratification of Bill of Rights, 61
- ratification of Constitution, 45–47
- size of, at time of Federal Convention, 20

Massachusetts Body of Liberties, 58, 63
*McCulloch* v. *Maryland*, 95
Milligan, L. P., 92
Mississippi, prohibition law, 72
Mississippi River, Spanish control of, 7–8
Money. *See* Paper money
Money bills, legislative branch's powers in, 25
- as envisioned by framers, 26, 32–33

Monroe, James, 48, 56

Morris, Gouverneur, at Federal Convention, 18, 28, 36, 39
Morris, Robert, 14

National American Women's Suffrage Association, 70
National Women's Suffrage Association, 70
Navigation Acts, 5–6
- of Confederation states, 6
Navigation rights, dispute over, during Confederation, 9
Necessary and Proper Clause, 34, 94–95, 101
Negative, definition of, 130
New Hampshire
- delegates to Federal Convention, 14, 103
- navigation acts, 6
- ratification of Bill of Rights, 60
- ratification of Constitution, 47–49
New Jersey
- delegates to Federal Convention, 19, 103
- position on legislative representation, at Federal Convention, 28
- ratification of Bill of Rights, 60
- reaction to New York's imposts, 8–9
New Jersey Plan, 20–22, 31
New York
- beliefs on congressional representation, 4
- claim to Western Territory, 7
- delegates to Federal Convention, 20–21, 28, 103
- importance of, to union, 50
- imposts, 8, 20
- navigation acts, 6
- ratification of Bill of Rights, 60
- ratification of Constitution, 41, 48, 50
- representation at Annapolis Convention, 9